KEYS
TO HIS
KINGDOM

KEYS TO HIS KINGDOM

Words of Wisdom from His Saints

Chuck Gross

Hickory Hill Press
Nashville, Tennessee

Nihil Obstat: REV. Justin N. Rains S.T.L.
Censor Librorum
Nashville, Tennessee 7 June 2024

Imprimatur: Very Rev. John J. H. Hammond, V.G.J.C.L.
Vicar General, Diocese of Nashville
Nashville, Tennessee 7 June 2024

The *Nihil Obstat* and *Imprimatur* are a declaration that a book or pamphlet is considered to be free from doctrinal or moral error.

The quotes and prayers used in this book are taken from the public domain or are copied under the Fair Use Doctrine, codified in 17 U.S.C.107.

Permissions:
hickoryhillpress@yahoo.com

Keys to His Kingdom is available at special quantity discounts for bulk purchase for church or school promotions, premiums, fund-raising, and educational needs. For details, write Hickory Hill Press Special Markets at hickoryhillpress@yahoo.com.

ISBN-13: 978-0-9839158-6-7

Cover design by Molly Gross

Cover photo of stained glass at Cathedral of Our Lady of Angels courtesy of Phillip Greenspan.

I dedicate this book to all the great saints, and especially St. Padre Pio and St. Gemma Galgani for their incredible intercessory help that my family and I have received from them.

"If you believe what you like in the Gospel, and reject what you don't like, it is not the Gospel you believe, but yourself."

St. Augustine

CONTENTS

INTRODUCTION

Your primary focus in life should be to save your soul. Salvation is not a one-time prayer where you accept Jesus as your savior and then you are guaranteed salvation. Oh, if it was that simple. In scripture, Jesus tells us, "If anyone wishes to come after me, he must deny himself and take up his cross daily and follow me." To follow Jesus, you must learn to unite your will with God's will. In our fallen condition this is not an easy thing to accomplish.

Obtaining one's salvation is a lifetime journey of ups and downs, of sins and repentance, of love and loss and especially of suffering both physically and emotionally. It is important to remember that Jesus teaches us, "I am the vine, you are the branches. Whoever remains in me and I in him will bear much fruit, because without me you can do nothing."

In my own journey, I have found the teachings of the blessed very rewarding in instructing us on how to live our lives as God wants us to, uniting our will with His. These teachings have motivated me in both my prayer and daily life. I realize that a lot of people do not have the time to spend reading the numerous books about the blessed, so I have picked out some of the quotes that I personally found helpful in my spiritual growth.

I have compiled these quotes in the hope that the reading of and the mediating on them will steer you on the right path to your salvation. These quotes are taken from the early Church Fathers, the Doctors of the Church, the canonized Saints, the Blessed and the Servants of God. They teach us how to, as the Holy Apostle said, "work out your salvation with fear and trembling." We know that these canonized saints have already obtained their salvation, and it is always better to learn from someone who has already obtained the knowledge that one is seeking.

Chapter 1

Angels

"For he will give his angels charge of you,
to guard you in all your ways.
On their hands they will bear you up,
lest you dash your foot against a stone."

Psalm 91:11-12

One of the most neglected resources that God has given his children to help them on their journey to salvation are the angels. We read in the Old Testament that the angels helped Abraham, Jacob, Elias, Daniel, Agar and Judith. In the New Testament we read how Peter and Paul were helped by the angels.

God has assigned each one of us our own personal guardian angel to watch over us and help us on our journey. The angels are always waiting to help us, but due to the nature of our free will, we must ask them for this help.

You should pray to your angel and ask for his guidance and protection. Ask him to make you aware of situations that lead you into sin.

In the lives of Saints Gemma Galgani and Padre Pio we read how they saw their guardian angels and would converse with them. Their angels would do errands for them and help guide them along their spiritual journey. Do not fail to take advantage of this great gift.

****

"You should know that there is present with you the angel whom God has appointed for each man. . . This angel, who is sleepless and cannot be deceived, is always present with you; he sees all things and is not hindered by darkness. You should know, too, that with him is God."

ST. ANTHONY OF EGYPT
Desert Father, 251-365

"If you are willing to listen to the Lord of the angels, my soul, you will have no reason to envy the angels their lofty place or how they move at tremendous speeds without tiring. For you will not only be equal to the angels when you are freed from the body, but also... you will possess together with your body heaven as your own home."

ST. JOHN BELLARIME
Cardinal, Doctor of the Church, 1542-1621

ANGELS

"He hath given his angels charge over thee." O wonderful bounty and truly great love of charity! Who? For whom? Wherefore? What has He commanded? Let us study closely, brethren, and let us diligently commit to our memory this great mandate. Who is it that commands? Whose angels are they? Whose mandates do they fulfill? Whose will do they obey? In answer, "He hath given his angels charge over thee, to keep thee in all thy ways." And they do not hesitate even to lift thee up in their hands...

"In this, therefore, brethren, let us affectionately love His angels as one day our future coheirs; meanwhile, however, as counselors and defenders appointed by the Father and placed over us. Why should we fear under such guardians? Those who keep us in all our ways can neither be overcome nor be deceived, much less deceive. They are faithful; they are prudent; they are powerful; why do we tremble? Let us only follow them, let us remain close to them, and in the protection of the God of heaven let us abide.

"As often, therefore, as a most serious temptation is perceived to weigh upon you and an excessive trial is threatening, call to your guard, your leader, your helper in your needs, in your tribulation; cry to him and say: "Lord, save us; we perish!" *The Holy Guardian Angels.*

ST. BERNARD OF CLAIRVAUX
Abbot, Doctor of the Church, 1090-1153

"The Devil writes down our sins - our Guardian Angel all our merits. Labor that the Guardian Angel's book may be full, and the Devil's empty."

3

KEYS TO HIS KINGDOM

"Our Guardian Angels are our most faithful friends, because they are with us day and night, always and everywhere. We ought often to invoke them."

ST. JOHN VIANNEY
Priest, 1786-1859

"Beside each believer stands an Angel as protector and shepherd, leading him to life."

ST. BASIL THE GREAT
Father and Doctor of the Church, 330-379

"Let us be like the holy angels now. ... If one day we are to be in the angelic court, we must learn how, while we are still here, the manners of the angels."

ST. VINCENT FERRER
Dominican preacher, 1350-1419

"I bind to myself today the power in the love of the Seraphim, in the obedience of the Angels, in the ministration of the Archangels, in the hope of Resurrection unto reward, in the prayers of the Patriarchs, in the predictions of the Prophets, in the preaching of the Apostles, in the faith of the Confessors, in the purity of the holy Virgins, in the deeds of Righteous men."

ST. PATRICK
Bishop, 385-461

ANGELS

"We should show our affection for the angels, for one day they will be our coheirs just as here below they are our guardians and trustees appointed and set over us by the Father."

ST. BERNARD OF CLAIRVAUX
Abbot, Doctor of the Church, 1090-1153

"Since God often sends us his inspirations by means of his angels, we ought frequently to offer him our aspirations through the same channel. ... Call on them and honor them frequently, and ask their help in all your affairs, temporal as well as spiritual."

ST. FRANCIS DE SALES
Bishop, Doctor of the Church, 1567-1622

"Be good. This will make your angel happy. When sorrows and misfortunes, physical or spiritual, afflict you, turn to your guardian angel with strong trust and he will help you."

"Be ever more convinced that your guardian angel is really present, that he is ever at your side. St. Frances of Rome always saw him standing before her, his arms clasped at his breast, his eyes uplifted to Heaven; but at the slightest failing, he would cover his face as if in shame, and at times, turn his back to her."

ST. JOHN BOSCO
Priest, 1815-1888

KEYS TO HIS KINGDOM

"Gemma saw her guardian angel with her own eyes, touched him with her hand, as if he were a being of this world, and would talk to him as would one friend to another. "Jesus" she once said. "Has not left me alone; He makes my guardian angel stay with me always." *The Life of St. Gemma Galgani.*

VENERABLE FATHER GERMANUS C.P.
1850-1909

"At the orders of the queen, the angels frequently assisted the apostles in their travels and tribulations ... The angels often visited them in visible shapes, conversing with them and consoling them in the name of the most blessed Mary."

VEN. MARY OF AGREDA
Nun, Abbess, Mystic, 1602-1665

"Cherubim means knowledge in abundance. They provide an everlasting protection for that which appeases God, namely, the calm of your heart, and they will cast a shadow of protection against all the attacks of malign spirits."

ST. JOHN CASSIAN
Monk, Mystic writer, Church Father, 360-435

"The powers of hell will assail the dying Christian; but his angel guardian will come to console him. His patrons, and St. Michael, who has been appointed by God to defend his faithful servants in their last combat with the devils, will come to his aid."

ST. ALPHONSUS LIGUORI
Bishop, Doctor of the Church, 1696-1787

Chapter 2

Pride

"But the soul that committeth anything through pride, whether he be born in the land or a stranger (because he hath been rebellious against the Lord) shall be cut off from among his people."

Number 15:30

Scripture and the blessed teach us that pride is one of the worst vices that will prevent one from attaining salvation. It takes away the glory that is due to our Creator. Instead of recognizing our nothingness (compared to God) which is essential for our salvation, pride strokes our ego and leads us to believe that we are special. Pride leads us to believe that everything we have accomplished is because of us and not of God. This robs

KEYS TO HIS KINGDOM

God of the glory due Him. Instead of giving the thanks and glory to God, we take it for ourselves believing that we are special and above the rest of God's children.

****

"We put pride into everything like salt. We like to see that our good works are known. If our virtues are seen, we are pleased; if our faults are perceived, we are sad. I remark that in a great many people; if one says anything to them, it disturbs them, it annoys them. The saints were not like that -- they were vexed if their virtues were known and pleased that their imperfections should be seen."

"Envy, my children, follows pride; whoever is envious is proud. See, envy comes to us from Hell; the devils having sinned through pride, sinned also through envy, envying our glory, our happiness. Why do we envy the happiness and the goods of others? Because we are proud; we should like to be the sole possessors of talents, riches, of the esteem and love of all the world! We hate our equals, because they are our equals; our inferiors, from the fear that they may equal us; our superiors, because they are above us."

ST. JOHN VIANNEY
Priest, 1786-1859

"Do not think yourself better than others lest, perhaps, you be accounted worse before God Who knows what is in man. Do not take pride in your good deeds, for God's

PRIDE

judgments differ from those of men and what pleases them often displeases Him."

"It is better for you to have little than to have much which may become the source of pride."

"I do not desire consolation that robs me of contrition, nor do I care for contemplation that leads to pride, for not all that is high is holy, nor is all that is sweet, good, nor every desire pure, nor all that is dear to us pleasing to God."

"Allow no pride to dwell in you but prove yourself so humble and lowly that all may walk over you and trample upon you as dust in the streets!" *The Imitation of Christ.*

THOMAS A KEMPAS
Priest, 1380-1471

"It was pride that changed angels into devils; it is humility that makes men as angels."

ST. AUGUSTINE
Bishop, Father and Doctor of the Church, 354-430

"The proud person is like a grain of wheat thrown into water: it swells, it gets big. Expose that grain to the fire: it dries up, it burns. The humble soul is like a grain of wheat thrown into the earth: it descends, it hides itself, it disappears, it dies; but to revive in heaven."

BL. MARY OF JESUS CRUCIFIED
Nun, Stigmatic, Mystic, Martyr, 1846-1878

KEYS TO HIS KINGDOM

"Above all feel ashamed of the pride of the human heart which does not wish to be subject, but always seeks to lord it over others and stand above them. And thus, the mind of those persons who are invited to the marriage of the lamb, that is to holy religion, are confounded for they believe that, after a short time during which they stood at the gate of salutary obedience, they are suitable to have the power to rule and manage others."

ST. CATHERINE OF BOLOGNA
Abbess, Mystic, Incorrupt, 1413-1463

"The greatest misery does not stop Me from uniting Myself to a soul, but where there is pride, I am not there." - Divine Mercy in my Soul (1563).

JESUS TO ST. FAUSTINA

"In prosperity, give thanks to God with humility and fear lest by pride you abuse God's benefits and so offend him."

ST. LOUIS IX
King of France, Crusader, 1214-1270

"For Thou art great, O Lord, and hast respect unto the humble, but the proud Thou beholdest afar off. Nor dost Thou draw near, but to the contrite in heart, nor art found by the proud, no, not though by curious skill they could number the stars and the sand, and measure the starry heavens, and track the courses of the planets."

ST. AUGUSTINE
Bishop, Father and Doctor of the Church, 354-430

PRIDE

"It is necessary to entertain a fear of the vice of pride. A priest, particularly, in order to preserve chastity, stands in need of special aid from God. "Pride," says the wise man, "is a sign of approaching ruin. The spirit is lifted up before the fall." (Prov 16:18). David, who, as he himself afterward confessed with tears, fell into adultery because he was not humble. "Before I was humbled, I offended." Psalm 118:67.

"Ask certain persons why they always fall back into the same impurities; pride shall answer for them, that it is the cause of their relapses. They are full of self-esteem, and there the Lord chastises them by permitting them to remain immersed in their abominations. "God gave them up to the desires of their heart, unto uncleanness, to dishonor their own bodies among themselves." Romans 1:24.

"Many often err and accomplish little or nothing because they try to become learned rather than to live well."

ST. BERNARD OF CLAIRVAUX
Abbot, Doctor of the Church, 1090-1153

"The devil has no fear of the proud. St. Joseph Calasanctius used to say that the devil treats a proud priest as a play-toy; that is, he throws him up and pulls him down as he pleases." *Dignity and Duties of the Priest.*

ST. ALPHONSUS LIGUORI
Bishop, Doctor of the Church, 1696-1787

11

KEYS TO HIS KINGDOM

"Pride corrodes grace. In the hearts of the proud there is nothing but a void all full of smoke, which produces blindness." *Book of Heaven,* Volume 3, November 3, 1899.

SERVANT OF GOD LUISA PICCARRETTA
Mystic, "Little Daughter of the Divine Will", 1865-1947

"Pride is the beginning of sin. And what is pride but the craving for undue exaltation? And this is undue exaltation - when the soul abandons Him to whom it ought to cleave as its end, and becomes a kind of end to itself." *City of God.*

ST. AUGUSTINE
Bishop, Father and Doctor of the Church, 354-430

"You must ask God to give you power to fight against the sin of pride which is your greatest enemy – the root of all that is evil, and the failure of all that is good. For God resists the proud."

ST. VINCENT DE PAUL
Priest, 1581-1660

"God resists the proud but give grace to the humble." James 3:6.

Chapter 3

Humility

"For everyone who exalts himself shall be humbled, and the one that humbles himself shall be exalted."

Luke 14: 11

There is no salvation without humility. The blessed teach us that humility is the greatest virtue to battle against pride. The demons hate it because it destroys the sin of pride which they choose when they fell. God loves the virtue of humility because it helps restore us to the natural order.

******

KEYS TO HIS KINGDOM

"The soul's true greatness is in loving God and in humbling oneself in His presence, completely forgetting oneself and believing oneself to be nothing; because the Lord is great, but He is well-pleased only with the humble; He always opposes the proud."

ST. FAUSTINA
Sister, Mystic, "Secretary of Divine Mercy", 1905-1938

On her deathbed, being asked by one of the nursing Sisters in attendance what virtue was the most important and dearest to God, Gemma answered, "Humility; humility is the foundation of all the others."

ST. GEMMA GALGANI
Mystic, Stigmatic, 1878-1903

"Humility is the foundation of all the other virtues hence, in the soul in which this virtue does not exist there cannot be any other virtue except in mere appearance."

ST. AUGUSTINE
Bishop, Father and Doctor of the Church, 354-430

"A truly humble person never believes that he can be wronged in anything. Truly, we ought to be shamed to resent whatever is said or done against us; for it is the greatest shame in the world to see that our Creator bears so many insults from His creatures, and that we resent even a little word that is contradictory."

ST. TERESA OF AVILA
Nun, First women Doctor of the Church, 1515-1582

HUMILITY

"The first degree of humility is the fear of God, which we should constantly have before our eyes."

ST. LOUIS DE BLOIS
Monk, Abbott, 1506-1566

"The most powerful weapon to conquer the devil is humility. For, as he does not know at all how to employ it, neither does he know how to defend himself from it."

ST. VINCENT DE PAUL
Priest, 1581-1660

"To be pleased at correction and reproofs shows that one loves the virtues which are contrary to those faults for which he is corrected and reproved. And, therefore, it is a great sign of advancement in perfection."

ST. FRANCIS DE SALES
Bishop, Doctor of the Church, 1567-1622

"To be taken with love for a soul, God does not look on its greatness, but the greatness of its humility."

ST. JOHN OF THE CROSS
Priest, Mystic, Doctor of the Church, 1542-1591

"We should let God be the One to praise us and not praise ourselves. For God detests those who commend themselves. Let others applaud our good deeds."

POPE ST. CLEMENT I
Bishop of Rome, Apostolic Father, 35AD-99AD

KEYS TO HIS KINGDOM

"Prayer must be humble: God resists the proud but gives grace to the humble. Here St. James tells us that God does not listen to the prayers of the proud, but resists them; while, on the other hand, he is always ready to hear the prayers of the humble: The prayer of the man that humbleth himself shall pierce the clouds, . . . and he will not depart till the Most High behold. The prayer of a humble soul at once penetrates the heavens and presents itself before the throne of God and will not depart thence till God regards it and listens to it. However sinful such a soul may be, God can never despise a heart that repents of its sins, and humbles itself: A contrite and humbled heart, O God, Thou wilt not despise."

ST. ALPHONSUS LIGUORI
Bishop, Doctor of the Church, 1696-1787

"For a man's merits are not to be estimated by his having many visions or consolations, nor by his knowledge in scriptures, nor by his being placed in a more elevated station. But by his being grounded in true humility and replenished with divine charity; by his seeking always purely and entirely the honor of God; by his esteeming himself as nothing and sincerely despising himself, and being better pleased to be despised and humbled by others than to be the object of their esteem." *The Imitation of Christ.*

THOMAS A KEMPAS
Priest, 1380-1471

HUMILITY

"In the difficulties which are placed before me, why should I not act like a donkey? When one speaks ill of him, the donkey says nothing. When he is mistreated, he says nothing. When he is forgotten, he says nothing. When no food is given him, he says nothing. When he is made to advance, he says nothing. When he is despised, he says nothing. When he is overburdened, he says nothing. The true servant of God must do likewise and say with David: "Before Thee I have become like a beast of burden."

ST. ALPHONSUS RODRIGUEZ
Brother, 1532-1617

"And all of you, clothe your-selves in your dealings with one another for; God opposes the proud but bestows favor on the humble." 1 Peter 5: 5.

"Humility is the key of the door of Heaven, such that no one can enter into It if she does not keep the key in good custody." *Book of Heaven,* Volume 3, January 12, 1900.

SERVANT OF GOD LUISA PICCARRETTA
Mystic, "Little Daughter of the Divine Will", 1865-1947

"Many of those who are humiliated are not humble, some react to humiliation with anger, others with patience, and others with freedom, the first are culpable, the next harmless, the last just."

ST. BERNARD OF CLAIRVAUX
Abbot, Doctor of the Church, 1090-1153

KEYS TO HIS KINGDOM

"Keep your heart in peace and let nothing trouble you, not even your faults. You must humble yourself and amend them peacefully, without being discouraged or cast down, for God's dwelling is in peace."

"Be humble towards God and gentle with your neighbor. Judge and accuse no one but yourself, and ever excuse others. Speak of God always to praise and glorify Him, speak of your neighbor only with respect -- do not speak of yourself at all, either well or ill."

ST. MARGARET MARY ALACOQUE
Nun, Mystic, Sacred Heart of Jesus devotion, 1647-1690

Prayer for Humility

O God, who resists the proud, and gives grace to the humble: grant us the virtue of true humility, where of Your Only begotten son showed in Himself a pattern for Your faithful; that we may never by our pride provoke Your anger, but rather by our meekness receive the riches. Amen.

Chapter 4

Anger and Hatred

"You know, my dearest brethren. And let every man be swift to hear, but slow to speak and slow to anger. For the anger of man worketh not the justice of God."

James 1:19-20

Anger is the door when left open allows hatred to come rushing in. We must be very careful of getting angry. Anger in itself is not always sinful, but as the blessed teach us, there is a fine line which is really easy to step over between righteous anger and sinful anger. Anger, when harbored, many times leads to hatred which against our fellow man is always sinful.

****

KEYS TO HIS KINGDOM

"Whosoever is angry with his brother shall be in danger of the judgment." Matthew 5:22

"A man who does not restrain the impulse of anger, easily falls into hatred towards the person who has been the occasion of his passion. According to St. Augustine, hatred is nothing else than persevering anger. Hence St. Thomas says that "anger is sudden, but hatred is lasting." (Opusc. v.) It appears, then, that in him in whom anger perseveres hatred also reigns."

ST. ALPHONSUS LIGUORI
Bishop, Doctor of the Church, 1696-1787

"It is better not to allow anger, however just and reasonable, to enter at all, than to admit it in ever so slight a degree; once admitted, it will not be easily expelled, for, though at first but a small plant, it will immediately grow into a large tree."

ST. AUGUSTINE
Bishop, Father and Doctor of the Church, 354-430

"There is no sin nor wrong that gives a man such a foretaste of hell in this life as anger and impatience. It is hated by God, it holds its neighbor in aversion, and has neither knowledge nor desire to bear and forbear with its faults. And whatever is said or done to it, it at once empoisons, and its impulses blow about like a leaf in the wind."

ST. CATHERINE OF SIENA
Doctor of the Church, Stigmatic, Mystic, 1347-1380

ANGER AND HATRED

"The memory of insults is the residue of anger. It keeps sins alive, hates justice, ruins virtue, poisons the heart, rots the mind, defeats concentration, paralyzes prayer, puts love at a distance, and is a nail driven into the soul. If anyone has appeased his anger, he has already suppressed the memory of insults, while as long as the mother is alive the son persists. In order to appease the anger, love is necessary."

ST. JOHN CLIMACUS
Monk, 579-649

"When you feel the assaults of passion and anger, then is the time to be silent as Jesus was silent in the midst of His ignominies and sufferings."

ST. PAUL OF THE CROSS
Priest, Founder of the Passionists, 1694-1775

"If, when stung by slander or ill-nature, we wax proud and swell with anger, it is a proof that our gentleness and humility are unreal, and mere artificial show."

"Most emphatically I say it, if possible, fall out with no one, and on no pretext, whatever suffer your heart to admit anger and passion. Saint James says, plainly and unreservedly, that "the wrath of man worketh not the righteousness of God."

ST. FRANCIS DE SALES
Bishop, Doctor of the Church, 1567-1622

KEYS TO HIS KINGDOM

"Take pains to refrain from sharp words. Pardon one another so that later on you will not remember the injury. The recollection of an injury is itself wrong. It adds to our anger, nurtures our sins and hates what is good. It is a rusty arrow and poison for the soul. It puts all virtue to flight."

ST. FRANCIS OF PAOLA
Friar, Founder of the Minim Friars, 1416-1507

"Dismiss all anger and look a little into yourself. Remember that he of whom you are speaking is your brother, and, as he is in the way of salvation, God can make him a Saint, notwithstanding his present weaknesses. You may fall into the same faults or perhaps into a worse fault. But supposing that you remain upright, to whom are you indebted for it, if not to the pure mercy of God?"

ST. THOMAS OF VILLANOVA
Archbishop, 1488-1555

"Do you ask how to resist anger? As soon as you feel the slightest resentment, gather together your powers, not hastily or impetuously, but gently and seriously. For as in some law courts, the criers make more noise in their efforts to preserve quiet than those they seek to still, so, if we are impetuous in our attempts to restrain our anger, we cause greater discomposure in our hearts than before; and once thrown off its balance, the heart is no longer its own master."

ST. FRANCIS DE SALES
Bishop, Doctor of the Church, 1567-1622

ANGER AND HATRED

"When you feel the assaults of passion and anger, then is the time to be silent as Jesus was silent in the midst of His ignominies and sufferings. O holy silence, rich in great virtues! O holy silence, which is a key of gold, keeping in safety the great treasure of holy virtues!"

ST. PAUL OF THE CROSS
Priest, Founder of the Passionists, 1694-1775

"The humble live in continuous peace, while in the hearts of the proud are envy and frequent anger."

"Grace looks to eternal things and does not cling to those which are temporal, being neither disturbed at loss nor angered by hard words, because she has placed her treasure and joy in heaven where nothing is lost."

THOMAS A KEMPAS
Priest, 1380-1471

"Be as gentle always as possible; and remember that you will catch more flies with a spoonful of honey than with a hundred barrels of vinegar. Such is the nature of the human mind; it rebels against severity, but gentleness renders it amenable to everything. A soft word appeases anger, as water extinguishes fire. No soul so ungrateful, but kindness can make it bear fruit. To speak truths sweetly is to throw burning coals, or rather roses, into a person's face. How can anyone be angry with another who fights him with pearls and diamonds?"

KEYS TO HIS KINGDOM

"Depend upon it, it is better to learn how to live without being angry than to imagine one can moderate and control anger lawfully; and if through weakness and frailty one is overtaken by it, it is far better to put it away forcibly than to parley with it; for give anger ever so little way, and it will become master, like the serpent, who easily works in its body wherever it can once introduce its head." *Introduction to the Devout Life.*

ST. FRANCIS DE SALES
Bishop, Doctor of the Church, 1567-1622

"Nothing is more powerful than meekness. For as fire is extinguished by water, so a mind inflated by anger is subdued by meekness. By meekness we practice and make known our virtue, and also cause the indignation of our brother to cease and deliver his mind from perturbation."

ST. JOHN CHRYSOSTOM
Archbishop, Father and Doctor of the Church, 347-407

"There is an anger which is engendered of evil, and there is an anger engendered of good. Hastiness of temper is the cause of the evil, divine principle is the cause of the good, such as that which Phinees felt when he allayed God's anger by the use of his own sword."

POPE ST. GREGORY THE GREAT
Father and Doctor of the Church, 540-604

ANGER AND HATRED

"When we have to reply to anyone who has insulted us, we should be careful to do it always with meekness. A soft answer extinguishes the fire of wrath. If we feel ourselves angry, it is better for us to be silent, because we should speak amiss; when we become tranquil, we shall see that all our words were culpable."

ST. ALPHONSUS LIGUORI
Bishop, Doctor of the Church, 1696-1787

"Many appear full of mildness and sweetness as long as everything goes their own way; but the moment any contradiction or adversity arises, they are in a flame, and begin to rage like a burning mountain. Such people as these are like red-hot coals hidden under ashes. This is not the mildness which Our Lord undertook to teach us in order to make us like unto Himself."

ST. BERNARD OF CLAIRVAUX
Abbot, Doctor of the Church, 1090-1153

"In order to avoid contention, never contradict anyone, except in case of sin or some danger to a neighbor; and when necessary to contradict others, and to oppose your opinion to theirs, do it with so much mildness and tact, as not to appear to do violence to their mind, for nothing is ever gained by taking up things with excessive warmth and hastiness."

ST. LOUIS IX
King of France, Crusader, 1214-1270

KEYS TO HIS KINGDOM

"There are two methods to subdue anger. First, that before a person undertakes to act, he places before his mind the contumelies and sufferings which he will likely encounter, and, by reflecting on the shame borne by our Saviour, prepares himself to bear them patiently. Secondly, when we behold the excesses of others, we direct our thoughts to our own excesses, by which we offend others. This consideration of our own faults will lead us to excuse those of others. For a person who piously considers that he also has something which others must bear patiently in him will be easily disposed to bear patiently injuries he receives from others."

POPE ST. GREGORY THE GREAT
Father and Doctor of the Church, 540-604

"It is better to err by excess of mercy than by excess of severity... Wilt thou become a Saint? Be severe to thyself but kind to others."

ST. JOHN CHRYSOSTOM
Archbishop, Father and Doctor of the Church, 347-407

"When you are insulted by someone or humiliated, guard against angry thoughts, lest they arouse a feeling of irritation, and so cut you off from love and place you in the realm of hatred."

ST. MAXIMOS THE CONFESSOR
Monk, 508-662

ANGER AND HATRED

"St. Jerome says that anger is the door by which all vices enter the soul... Anger precipitates men into resentments, blasphemies, acts of injustice, detractions, scandals, and other iniquities; for the passion of anger darkens the understanding, and makes a man act like a beast and a madman. " Caligavit ab indignatione oculus meus." (Job xvii. 7.) My eye has lost its sight through indignation... Hence, according to St. Bonaventure, an angry man is incapable of distinguishing between what is just and unjust."

ST. ALPHONSUS LIGUORI
Bishop, Doctor of the Church, 1696-1787

Prayers to Help Anger

God, grant me the serenity to accept the things I cannot change, courage to change the things I can, and wisdom to know the difference. Amen.

Gentle Father, as this day comes to a conclusion, I beg You to take my anger and replace it with serenity. Take away my frustration and renew my belief in You. Help me to maintain my gentleness and compassion under pressure. Fill my heart with kindness rather than hostility, humility rather than anger, and faith rather than resentment. Through Christ our Lord. Amen.

Chapter 5

Gossip and Slander

"The lips of the arrogant talk of what is not their concern, but the discreet carefully weigh their words.

The mind of fools is in their mouths, but the mouth of the wise is in their mind.

When the godless curse their adversary, they really curse themselves.

Slanderers sully themselves, and are hated by their neighbors."

Ben Sira (Ecclesiasticus)

21:25-28

KEYS TO HIS KINGDOM

Gossip is one of those sins that most people today are not even aware of its sinfulness. The devil enjoys gossipers because gossip is very contagious and can easily turn into slander. How many times have you been listening to someone talking about someone that you don't particularly care for and before you know it, you're joining in in trashing that person. It is really easy to start repeating gossip that we have heard about that person not even knowing if what we are repeating is true. How God hates this. Saint Peter teaches us; "Whoever desires to love life and see good days, let him keep his tongue from evil and his lips from speaking deceit." (1 Peter 3: 10). How hard it is to restore a good name to someone who has been slandered.

****

"If something uncharitable is said in your presence, either speak in favor of the absent, or withdraw, or if possible, stop the conversation."

ST. JOHN VIANNEY
Priest, 1786-1859

"When you hear ill of anyone, refute the accusation if you can in justice do so; if not, apologize for the accused on account of his intentions ... and thus gently check the conversation, and if you can, mention something else favorable to the accused."

ST. FRANCIS DE SALES
Bishop, Doctor of the Church, 1567-1622

GOSSIP AND SLANDER

"The tongue of the scandalmonger is like the worm which gnaws at the good fruit --- that is, the best actions that people do --- and tries to turn them all to bad account. The tongue of the scandalmonger is a grub which taints the most beautiful of the flowers and upon them leaves behind it the disgusting trace of its own slime."

"There is yet another form of wrongdoing which is all the more deplorable in that it is more common, and that is licentious talk. There is nothing more abominable, my dear brethren, nothing more horrible than such talk... It outrages God, it scandalizes our neighbor."

"Very often it requires only one immodest or unseemly word to start a thousand evil thoughts, a thousand shameful desires, perhaps even to cause a fall into an infinite number of sins and to bring innocent souls evil of which they had been happily ignorant."

ST. JOHN VIANNEY
Priest, 1786-1859

"He who unjustly takes away his neighbor's good name is guilty of sin and is bound to make restitution."

"To speak ill of anyone, except from a motive of justice, is a mortal sin; and, to speak ill of a person who is absent, is a sin that contains a circumstance of great malignity."

KEYS TO HIS KINGDOM

"If you have been guilty of the sin of detraction, you are bound to restore the honor of the person whose character you have injured."

"Let it be your care always to speak well of all. Speak of others as you would wish to be spoken of by others. With regard to the absent, observe the excellent rule of St. Mary Magdalene de Pazzi: "Never to utter in their absence what you would not say in their presence.""

ST. ALPHONSUS LIGUORI
Bishop, Doctor of the Church, 1696-1787

"So also, the tongue is a small member, yet it boasts of great things. How great a forest is set ablaze by such a small fire." James 3:5.

"If anyone thinks he is religious and does not bridle his tongue but deceives his heart, this person's religion is worthless." James 1:26.

"A gentle tongue is a tree of life, but perverseness in it breaks the spirit." Proverbs 15:4.

"To the extent that you pray with all your soul for the person who slanders you, God will make the truth known to those who have been scandalized by the slander."

GOSSIP AND SLANDER

"Slander is a poison which kills charity, both in the slanderer and the one who listens."

"The spiteful tongue strikes a deadly blow at charity in all who hear him speak and, so far as it can, destroys root and branch, not only in the immediate hearers but also in all others to whom the slander, flying from lip to lip, is afterwards repeated."

ST. BERNARD OF CLAIRVAUX
Abbot, Doctor of the Church, 1090-1153

"If, when stung by slander or ill-nature, we wax proud and swell with anger, it is a proof that our gentleness and humility are unreal, and mere artificial show."

"While extremely sensitive as to the slightest approach to slander, you must also guard against an extreme into which some people fall, who, in their desire to speak evil of no one, actually uphold and speak well of vice."

"Never forget that souls are poisoned through the ear as much as bodies through the mouth."

ST. FRANCIS DE SALES
Bishop, Doctor of the Church, 1567-1622

"No passion is worse than an uncontrolled tongue, because it is the mother of all the passions."

ST. AGATHON
Pope, 577-681

KEYS TO HIS KINGDOM

"Blessed the one who loves truth continually and has not lent his mouth as an instrument of impiety by lying, for he fears the commandment about idle speech."

ST. EPHREM OF SYRIA
Doctor of the Church, Theologian, 306-373

"The Christian ought not to say anything behind his brother's back with the object of calumniating him, for this is slander, even if what is said is true. He ought to turn away from the brother who speaks evil against him?"

"One should not speak idle talk, for it is neither useful to those who listen, nor necessary or permissible with regard to God."

ST. BASIL THE GREAT
Father and Doctor of the Church, 330-379

"Blessed the one who loves good and fair words and hates base and destructive speech, because he will not become a prisoner of the Evil One."

"He who gives way to lying does so under the pretext of prudence, and he often regards what is the destruction of his soul as an act of righteousness. The inventor of lies makes out that he is an imitator of Rahab, and says that by his own destruction, he is affecting the salvation of others."

ST. JOHN CLIMACUS
Monk, 579-649

Chapter 6

Divorce

"For this reason a man shall leave his father and mother and be joined to his wife, and the two shall become one flesh'? So they are no longer two, but one flesh. Therefore, what God has joined together, let no one separate."

Matthew 19:5-6

Remarriage after divorce is one of those grievous sins that many Christians seem to ignore. Recent studies show anywhere between forty to fifty percent of marriages in the United Sates end up in divorce. Jesus told us in Matthew: He said to them, "Because of the hardness of your hearts Moses allowed you to divorce your wives, but from the beginning it was not so."(Mathew 19:8). Several of the protestant churches have given into the hardness of their parishioner's hearts and disregarding Jesus's own words have allowed divorce. What an affront to Jesus!

KEYS TO HIS KINGDOM

How many souls will be led astray and condemned to the eternal fire because of this selfishness? If you're one of these unfortunate individuals who has been granted a divorce in the past and has since remarried, salvation is not lost. Humble yourself and get to confession immediately. Check with your priest or pastor and see if you have proper grounds for a declaration of nullity, commonly known to a lay person as an annulment, of your first marriage. If that is not the case, you and your spouse can resolve to live as brother and sister refraining from sexual intercourse thus ending the adultery. Just remember that life is short and there is no end to the suffering of souls who go to Hell.

****

"What then shall the husband do, if the wife continues in this disposition [adultery]? Let him divorce her, and let the husband remain single. But if he divorces his wife and marry another, he too commits adultery." *The Shepherd* 4:1:6 (A.D. 80).

HERMAS
First Century Author

"Just as a woman is an adulteress, even though she seems to be married to a man, while a former husband yet lives, so also the man who seems to marry her who has been divorced does not marry her, but, according to the declaration of our Savior, he commits adultery with her." *Commentaries on Matthew* 14:24 (A.D. 248).

DIVORCE

"A man who marries after another man's wife has been taken away from him will be charged with adultery in the case of the first woman; but in the case of the second he will be guiltless." *Second Canonical Letter to Amphilochius* 199:37 (375 A.D.).

ST. BASIL THE GREAT
Father and Doctor of the Church, 330-379

"No one is permitted to know a woman other than his wife. The marital right is given you for this reason: lest you fall into the snare and sin with a strange woman. 'If you are bound to a wife do not seek a divorce'; for you are not permitted, while your wife lives, to marry another." (*Abraham* 1:7:59 (A.D. 387).

"You dismiss your wife as if by right and without being charged with wrongdoing; and you suppose it is proper for you to do so because no human law forbids it; but divine law forbids it. Anyone who obeys men ought to stand in awe of God. Hear the law of the Lord, which even they who propose our laws must obey: "What God has joined together let no man put asunder." – *Commentary on Luke* 8:5 (A.D. 389).

ST. AMBROSE
Bishop, Father and Doctor of the Church, 339-397

"Do not tell me about the violence of the ravisher, about the persuasiveness of a mother, about the authority of a father, about the influence of relatives, about the intrigues and insolence of servants, or about household

financial] losses. So long as a husband lives, be he
adulterer, be he sodomite, be he addicted to every kind
of vice, if she left him on account of his crimes, he is her
husband still and she may not take another." *Letters*
55:3 (A.D. 396).

"Wherever there is fornication and a suspicion of
fornication, a wife is freely dismissed. Because it is
always possible that someone may calumniate the
innocent and, for the sake of a second joining in
marriage, act in criminal fashion against the first, it is
commanded that when the first wife is dismissed, a
second may not be taken while the first lives."
Commentaries on Matthew 3:19:9 (A.D. 398).

ST. JEROME
Priest, Father and Doctor of the Church, 1347-1420

"The practice is observed by all of regarding as an
adulteress a woman who marries a second time while her
husband yet lives, and permission to do penance is not
granted her until one of them is dead." *Letters* 2:13:15
(A.D. 408).

POPE INNOCENT I
Died 417

"A woman begins to be the wife of no later husband
unless she has ceased to be the wife of a former one. She
will cease to be the wife of a former one, however, if that
husband should die, not if he commit fornication. A
spouse, therefore, is lawfully dismissed for cause of

38

DIVORCE

fornication; but the bond of chastity remains. That is why a man is guilty of adultery if he marries a woman who has been dismissed even for this very reason of fornication." *Adulterous Marriages* 2:4:4.

"Undoubtedly the substance of the sacrament is of this bond, so that when man and woman have been joined in marriage they must continue inseparably as long as they live, nor is it allowed for one spouse to be separated from the other except for cause of fornication. For this is preserved in the case of Christ and the Church, so that, as a living one with a living one, there is no divorce, no separation forever." *Marriage and Concupiscence* 1:10:11 (A.D. 419).

ST. AUGUSTINE
Bishop, Father and Doctor of the Church, 354-430

"My daughter, this is why I am calling you to sufferings again – so that, as you offer yourself with Me to Divine Justice, those who must fight this law of divorce may obtain light and efficacious grace in order to be victorious. My daughter, I tolerate that they make wars and revolutions, and that the blood of the new martyrs inundate the world – this is an honor for Me and for my Church; but this brutal law (allowing divorce) is an affront to my Church, and it is abominable and intolerable to Me." *Book of Heaven Vol*ume 4, January 12, 1902.

JESUS TO LUISA PICCARRETA

KEYS TO HIS KINGDOM

"That Scripture counsels marriage, however, and never allows any release from the union, is expressly contained in the law: 'You shall not divorce a wife, except for reason of immorality.' And it regards as adultery the marriage of a spouse, while the one from whom a separation was made is still alive. 'Whoever takes a divorced woman as wife commits adultery,' it says; for 'if anyone divorce his wife, he debauches her'; that is, he compels her to commit adultery. And not only does he that divorces her become the cause of this, but also, he that takes the woman and gives her the opportunity of sinning; for if he did not take her, she would return to her husband." *Miscellanies* 2:23:145:3 (A.D. 208).

ST. CLEMENT OF ALEXANDRIA
Father of the Church, 150-215

"Concerning chastity, [Jesus] uttered such sentiments as these: "Whosoever looks upon a woman to lust after her, has committed adultery with her already in his heart before God." And, "If your right eye offends you, cut it out, for it is better for you to enter into the kingdom of heaven with one eye, than, having two eyes, to be cast into everlasting fire." And, "Whosoever shall marry her that is divorced from another husband commits adultery." And, "There are some who have been made eunuchs of men, and some who were born eunuchs, and some who have made themselves eunuchs for the kingdom of heaven's sake; but all cannot receive this saying" [Mt 19:12]. So that all who, by human law, are twice married, and those who look upon a woman to lust after her, are in the eye of our master sinners. For not

DIVORCE

only he who in act commits adultery is rejected by him, but also, he who desires to commit adultery: since not only our works, but also our thoughts, are open before God." *First Apology* 15 (A.D. 151).

ST. JUSTIN MARTYR
Martyr, Christian Apologist and Philosopher, 100-165

Chapter 7

Temptations

"Keep watch and pray, all of you, so that you may not slip into temptation. The spirit indeed is eager but human nature is weak."

Mark 14:38

To grow in your spiritual life, you must discover your own weaknesses and learn to avoid the occasions that cause you to fall. By doing an examination of conscience every evening, you can discover where and when most of your sins are taking place. Take this information and apply it to your daily routine, teaching yourself to avoid those situations in which you tend to fall into sin. If these situations occur where they cannot be avoided, such as at work or school, you can seek advice from your spiritual counselor and pray and plan beforehand on how to handle these situations without sinning.

****

"For heavenly comfort is promised to such as have been proved by temptation. "To him that overcometh," saith Our Lord, 'I will give to eat of the tree of life." (Apoc. 2:7)." *The Imitation of Christ.*

THOMAS A KEMPAS
Priest, 1380-1471

"The greatest of all evils is not to be tempted, because then there are grounds for believing that the devil looks upon us as his property."

ST. JOHN VIANNEY
Priest, 1786-1859

"The Devil tempts so that he may ruin; God tests so that he may crown."

ST. AMBROISE OF MILAN
Bishop, Doctor of the Church, 339-397

"Whatever good is to be attained, struggle is necessary. So don't fear temptations, but rejoice in them, for they lead to achievement. God helps and protects you."

ST. BARSANUPHIUS OF GAZA
Hermit, unknown -545

TEMPTATIONS

"So, you will ask me, who then are the people most tempted? They are these, my friends; note them carefully. The people most tempted are those who are ready, with the grace of God, to sacrifice everything for the salvation of their poor souls, who renounce all those things, which most people eagerly seek. It is not one devil only who tempts them, but millions seek to entrap them."

ST. JOHN VIANNEY
Priest, 1786-1859

"Stop entertaining those vain fears. Remember it is not feeling which constitutes guilt but the consent to such feelings. Only the free will is capable of good or evil. But when the will sighs under the trial of the tempter and does not will what is presented to it, there is not only no fault but there is virtue."

PADRE PIO
Stigmatic, Mystic, 1897-1968

"When tempted, invoke your guardian angel. Ignore the Devil and do not be afraid of him. He trembles and flees at the sight of your guardian angel."

ST. JOHN BOSCO
Priest, 1815-1888

"There are in truth three states of the converted: the beginning, the middle, and the perfection. In the beginning they experience the charms of sweetness; in the middle the contests of temptation; and in the end the fullness of perfection."

KEYS TO HIS KINGDOM

"If some shameful thought is sown in your heart as you are sitting in your cell, watch out. Resist evil, so that it does not gain control over you. Make every effort to call God to mind, for He is looking at you, and whatever you are thinking in your heart is plainly visible to Him. Say to your soul: "If you are afraid of sinners like yourself seeing your sins, how much more should you be afraid of God who notes everything?" As a result of this warning the fear of God will be revealed in your soul, and if you cleave to Him you will not be shaken by the passions; for it is written: "They that trust in the Lord shall be as Mount Zion; he that dwells in Jerusalem shall never be shaken" (Ps. 125:1. LXX). Whatever you are doing, remember that God sees all your thoughts, and then you will never sin. To Him be glory through all the ages. Amen."

ST. ISAIAH THE SOLITARY
Monk, unknown-491

"Job was turned over to the Devil to be tempted so that, by withstanding the test. Job would become a torment to the Devil."

ST. AUGUSTINE
Bishop, Father and Doctor of the Church, 354-430

"Guard your mind, and you will not be harassed by temptations. But if you fail to guard it, accept patiently whatever trial comes."

ST. MARK THE ASCETIC
Monk, 360-430

TEMPTATIONS

"Do not grieve over the temptations you suffer. When the Lord intends to bestow a particular virtue on us, He often permits us first to be tempted by the opposite vice. Therefore, look upon every temptation as an invitation to grow in a particular virtue and a promise by God that you will be successful, if only you stand fast."

ST. PHILIP NERI
Priest, "Second Apostle of Rome", 1515-1595

"Trials are nothing else but the forge that purifies the soul of all its imperfections."

ST. MARY MAGDALEN DE'PAZZI
Nun. Mystic, Uncorrupt, 1566-1607

"However, we must be watchful, especially in the beginning of temptation, because then the enemy is easier overcome, if he is not suffered to come in at all at the door of the soul but is kept out and resisted at his first knock."

"For first a bare thought comes to the mind; then a strong imagination; afterwards delight, and evil motion and consent. And thus, by little and little, the wicked enemy gets full entrance, when he is not resisted in the beginning."

THOMAS A KEMPAS
Priest, 1380-1471

KEYS TO HIS KINGDOM

"God permits that kind of temptation in order to impress you with a deeper sense of your own nothingness, and to convince you that, deprived of His grace, you would be capable of committing the most heinous crimes. Therefore, act prudently, avoid all dangerous intercourse, watch over your eyes, your heart, and all your affections; be very modest, be circumspect in all your actions, by night as well as by day; love holy modesty."

ST. PAUL OF THE CROSS
Priest, Founder of the Passionists, 1694-1775

"The devil is like a rabid dog tied to a chain; beyond the length of the chain, he cannot seize anyone. And you: keep at a distance. If you approach too near, you let yourself be caught. Remember that the devil has only one door by which to enter the soul: the will."

PADRE PIO
Stigmatic, Mystic, 1897-1968

"Above all, it is necessary to ask God every morning the gift of perseverance, and to beg of the Blessed Virgin to obtain it for you, and particularly in the times of temptation, by invoking the name of Jesus and Mary as long as the temptation lasts."

ST. ALPHONSUS LIGUORI
Bishop, Doctor of the Church, 1696-1787

TEMPTATIONS

"Therefore, patience, humiliation, and offering God what one suffers in time of temptation is nourishing bread that one gives our Lord which He accepts with great pleasure." *The Book of Heaven*, Volume 2, September 30, 1899.

SERVANT OF GOD LUISA PICCARRETTA
Mystic, "Little Daughter of the Divine Will", 1865-1947

A Prayer Against Temptations

Lord Jesus Christ, Who was conducted as a criminal to the house of Annas, grant that I may never suffer myself to be led into sin by temptations of the evil spirit, or the evil suggestions of my fellow creatures, but that I may be securely guided by the Divine Spirit in the perfect accomplishment of Thy holy ordinances. Amen.

Chapter 8

Sinful Habits

"Put to death, then, the parts of you that are earthly: immorality, impurity, passion, evil desire, and the greed that is idolatry. Because of these the wrath of God is coming [upon the disobedient]. By these you too once conducted yourselves, when you lived in that way. But now you must put them all away: anger, fury, malice, slander, and obscene language out of your mouths. Stop lying to one another, since you have taken off the old self with its practices and have put on the new self, which is being renewed, for knowledge, in the image of its creator."

Colossians 3: 5-10

KEYS TO HIS KINGDOM

Saint Alphonsus Liguori, in his *Sermon Twenty* for Palm Sunday, uses three points to explain the evil effects of bad habits.
First point. A bad habit blinds the understanding.
Second point. It hardens the heart.
Third point. It diminishes our strength.'

He goes on to tell us, "Of those who live in the habit of sin, St. Augustine says: "Ipsa consuetudo non sinit videre malum, quod faciunt." The habit of sin blinds sinners, so that they no longer see the evil which they do, nor the ruin which they bring upon themselves; hence they live in blindness, as if there was neither God, nor Heaven, nor Hell, nor eternity. "Sins," adds the saint, "however enormous, when habitual, appear to be small, or not to be sins at all." How then can the soul guard against them, when she is no longer sensible of their deformity, or the evil which they bring upon her?"

****

"Whenever you feel guilty, even if it is because you have consciously committed a sin, a serious sin, something you have kept doing many, many times, never let the devil deceive you by allowing him to discourage you. Whenever you feel guilty, offer all your guilt to the Immaculate, without analyzing it or examining it, as something that belongs to her..."

"My beloved, may every fall, even if it is serious and habitual sin, always become for us a small step toward a higher degree of perfection."

SINFUL HABITS

'The devil, instead, tries to inject in us discouragement and internal depression in those circumstances, which is, in fact, nothing else than our pride surfacing again."

ST. MAXIMILIAN KOLBE
Friar, Martyr, 1894-1941

"These persons, I say, make their first attack against the beasts that they have noticed are stronger and fiercer, and when these have been killed, they more easily destroy the ones that are left, which are less terrible and less aggressive. Likewise, it is always the case that when the more powerful vices have been overthrown and are succeeded by weaker ones, we shall obtain a perfect victory without any hardship."

ST. JOHN CASSIAN
Monk, Mystic writer, Church Father, 360-435

"And when I hear it said that God is good and He will pardon us, and then see that men cease not from evil-doing, oh, how it grieves me! The infinite goodness with which God communicates with us, sinners as we are, should constantly make us love and serve Him better; but we, on the contrary, instead of seeing in his goodness an obligation to please Him, convert it into an excuse for sin which will of a certainty lead in the end to our deeper condemnation."

ST. CATHERINE OF GENOA
Lay person, Mystic, 1447-1510

KEYS TO HIS KINGDOM

"When we are in sin, our soul is all diseased, all rotten; it is pitiful. The thought that the good God sees it ought to make it enter into itself. And then, what pleasure is there in sin? None at all. We have frightful dreams that the devil is carrying us away, that we are falling over precipices. Put yourself on good terms with God; have recourse to the Sacrament of Penance; you will sleep as quietly as an angel. You will be glad to waken in the night, to pray to God; you will have nothing but thanksgivings on your lips; you will rise towards Heaven with great facility, as an eagle soars through the air."

ST. JOHN VIANNEY
Priest, 1786-1859

"Almost every sin is committed for the sake of sensual pleasure; and sensual pleasure is overcome by hardship and distress arising either voluntarily from repentance, or else involuntarily as a result of some salutary and providential reversal. 'For if we would judge ourselves, we should not be judged; but when we are judged, we are chastened by the Lord, so that we should not be condemned with the world'." (1 Cor. 11:31-32).

ST. MAXIMOS THE CONFESSOR
Monk, 508-662

"Satisfaction consists in the cutting off of the causes of the sin. Thus, fasting is the proper antidote to lust; prayer to pride, to envy, anger and sloth; alms to covetousness."

ST. RICHARD OF CHICHESTER
Bishop, 1198-1253

SINFUL HABITS

"I am not ignorant of what is said of my Lord in the Psalm: 'You destroy those who speak a lie.' And again: 'A lying mouth deals death to the soul.' And likewise, the Lord says in the Gospel: 'On the day of judgment men shall render account for every idle word they utter."

ST. PATRICK
Bishop, 385-461

"The signs that accompany those who wish to submit to the Logos of God and who bring forth good fruit are: sighing, weeping, sorrow, stillness, shaking of the head, prayer, silence, persistence, bitter grief, tribulation of heart arising from religious devotion. In addition, their actions manifest vigilance, fasting, self-control, gentleness, forbearance, unceasing prayer, study of the divine Scriptures, faith, humility, brotherly affection, submission, rigorous toil, hardship, love, kindliness, courtesy and-the sum of all-light, which is the Lord."

"The signs that accompany those who are not producing the fruit of life are listlessness, day-dreaming, curiosity, lack of attention, grumbling, instability; and in their actions they manifest gluttony, anger, wrath, back-biting, conceit, untimely talk, unbelief, disorderliness, forgetful-ness, unrest, sordid greed, avarice, envy, factiousness, contempt, garrulity, senseless laughter, willfulness and - the sum of all - darkness, which is Satan."

ST. SYMEON METAPHRASTES
Monk, Greek writer, 900-after 984

Chapter 9

Grievous (Mortal) Sins

"Mortal sin is a sin whose object is grave matter and which is also committed with full knowledge and deliberate consent."

If you want to advance in your spiritual life, you must be able to discern between venial and mortal sins. Jesus tells us in Matthew 5: 19,"Therefore, whoever breaks one of the least of these commandments and teaches men so, shall be called least in the kingdom of heaven; but he who does them and teaches them shall be called great in the kingdom of heaven." This shows us that there are sins that we can commit that do not break our relations ship with God and thus send us to perdition.

The Church calls these types of sins venial (not deadly) sins. The Catechism states: "Venial sin weakens charity...

57

and... merits temporal punishment. Deliberate and unrepented venial sin disposes us little by little to commit mortal sin. However, venial sin does not break the covenant with God. With God's grace, it is humanly reparable. "Venial sin does not deprive the sinner of sanctifying grace, friendship with God, charity, and consequently, eternal happiness." (CCC 1863).

This is not the case for mortal (deadly) sins. When you commit a mortal sin, you break off your relationship with God and instead of being a child of God you become a child of Satan. This is why it is imperative to immediately ask God for forgiveness, then get to confession as soon as possible and especially before receiving the Eucharist.

The Church teaches; "Mortal Sin destroys charity in the heart of man by a grave violation of God's law; it turns man away from God... by preferring an inferior good to him. Venial sin allows charity to subsist, though it offends and wounds it." (CCC 1855). "Mortal sin... results in... the privation of sanctifying grace, that is, of the state of grace. If it is not redeemed by repentance and God's forgiveness, it causes exclusion from Christ's kingdom and the eternal death of hell..." (CCC 1861).

****

"St. Augustine and St. Thomas define mortal sin to be a turning away from God: that is, the turning of one's back upon God, leaving the Creator for the sake of the creature. What punishment would that subject deserve who, while his king was giving him a command, contemptuously turned his back upon him to go and transgress his orders? This is what the sinner does; and

GREVIOUS (MORTAL) SINS

this is punished in hell with the pain of loss, that is, the loss of God, a punishment richly deserved by him who in this life turns his back upon his sovereign good."

"Let us now proceed. We have spoken of the examination regarding mortal and venial sins. But were a person to do an action with a doubt whether it was a mortal or a venial sin, what kind of sin would he commit? He would be guilty of mortal sin, because he exposes himself to the danger of grievously offending God. Hence, before he acts he must lay aside the doubt; and if he has not hitherto done so, he must confess it, at least, as it is before God. But the scrupulous, who have doubts about everything, must follow another rule: they must obey their confessor. When he tells them to conquer their doubts, and to act against scruples, they should obey with exactness; otherwise they will render themselves unable and unfit to perform any spiritual exercise."

ST. ALPHONSUS LIGUORI
Bishop, Doctor of the Church, 1696-1787

"Just as a disorder which destroys the principle of the body's life causes the body's death, so too a disorder which destroys the principle of spiritual life, viz. the last end, causes spiritual death, which is mortal sin." *Summa Theologiae*, Q. 74.

"Without sanctifying grace, it is not possible to refrain long from mortal sin." "I cannot understand how anyone conscious of mortal sin can laugh or be merry."

ST. THOMAS AQUINAS
Angelic Doctor of the Church, 1225-1274

KEYS TO HIS KINGDOM

"This I say, because God showed me somewhat of his truth, in order that I might know what man is without him; that is, when the soul is found in mortal sin, at that time, it is so monstrous and horrible to behold, that it is impossible to imagine anything equally so."

"I repeat it; all works, without the help of grace are dead, being produced by the creature only; but grace aids all works performed by those who are not in mortal sin and makes them worthy of heaven; not those which are ours solely, but those in which grace cooperates."

ST. CATHERINE OF GENOA
Lay person, Mystic, 1447-1510

"But if you take pleasure in committing even a slight sin, which you know to be a sin, and you do so trusting to your own abstinence and presuming on grace, without doing penance and reparation for it, know that it can become a mortal sin." *The Revelations of St. Bridget of Sweden.*

JESUS TO ST. BRIDGET

"Half-instructed confessors have done my soul great harm; for I could not always have such learned ones as I would have desired. They certainly did not wish to deceive me, but the fact was that they knew no better. Of something which was a venial sin, they said it was no sin, and out of a very grave mortal sin they made a venial sin. This has done me such harm, that my speaking here of so great an evil, as a warning to others, will be readily understood."

GREVIOUS (MORTAL) SINS

"I once heard a spiritual man say that he was not so much astonished at the things done by a soul in mortal sin as at the things not done by it. May God, in his mercy, deliver us from such great evil, for there is nothing in the whole of our lives that so thoroughly deserves to be called evil as this, since it brings endless and eternal evils in its train."

ST. TERESA OF JESUS
Nun, First women Doctor of the Church, 1515-1582

"We should all realize that no matter where or how a man dies, if he is in the state of mortal sin and does not repent, when he could have done so and did not, the Devil tears his soul from his body with such anguish and distress that only a person who has experienced it can appreciate it."

ST. FRANCES OF ASSISI
Friar, Mystic, Stigmatic, 1181-1226

"And when children begin to use their reason, fathers and mothers should take great pains to fill their hearts with the fear of God. This the good Queen Blanche did most earnestly by St. Louis, her son: witness her oft-repeated words, "My son, I would sooner see you die than guilty of a mortal sin;" words which sank so deeply into the saintly monarch's heart, that he himself said there was no day on which they did not recur to his mind, and strengthen him in treading God's ways."

ST. FRANCIS DE SALES
Bishop, Doctor of the Church, 1567-1622

KEYS TO HIS KINGDOM

"Yes, dear reader, before your Baptism you were a member of Satan, and now you are a member of Jesus Christ; you were a child of the devil, and now you are the child of God; you were a base associate of Satan, and you have become the sacred spouse of the Holy Ghost; you were the inheritor of the pains of hell, and now you are the heir of heaven; you were separated from your God, and you are united to him in most intimate union. Behold what you are, if you have still preserved the grace of your Baptism. But, alas! if you have lost it through mortal sin, the holy union which you contracted with God is broken."

ST. JEAN EUDES
Priest, 1601-1680

"Although the sinner does not believe in Hell, he shall nevertheless go there if he has the misfortune to die in mortal sin."

ST. ANTHONY MARY CLARET
Archbishop, Missionary,1807-1870

Chapter 10

Prayer

"And I tell you, ask and you will receive; seek and you will find; knock and the door will be opened to you. For everyone who asks, receives; and the one who seeks, finds; and to the one who knocks, the door will be opened. What father among you would hand his son a snake when he asks for a fish? Or hand him a scorpion when he asks for an egg? If you then, who are wicked, know how to give good gifts to your children, how much more will the Father in heaven give the holy Spirit to those who ask him?"

John 11: 9-13

Why must one pray? First, is because we owe it to God as our Creator to praise Him and thank Him for all He

KEYS TO HIS KINGDOM

has done for us in creation. Secondly, how can one expect to have a relationship with God if we never communicate with Him or think about Him. It is very important in developing a lovely relationship with God that on first awakening you develop the habit of praying. As you give your loved ones a kiss in the morning, do the same with God. Then at bedtime do the same. Do not forget to include the Blessed Mother and your guardian angel.

****

"In prayer one must learn to quiet themselves and listen, for silence is the language of God."

A SERVANT OF GOD

"Prayer is the raising of one's mind and heart to God or the requesting of good things from God." *De Fide Orth.* 3, 24.

ST. JOHN DAMASCENE
Priest, Father and Doctor of the Church, 676-749

"As the body without the soul cannot love, so the soul without prayer is dead and emits an offensive odor."

ST. JOHN CHRYSOSTOM
Archbishop, Father and Doctor of the Church, 347-407

"Pray, Hope, and Don't Worry."

PADRE PIO
Stigmatic, Mystic, 1897-1968

PRAYER

"While I was saying the chaplet [of Divine Mercy], I heard a voice which said, Oh, what great graces I will grant to souls who say this chaplet; the very depths of My tender mercy are stirred for the sake of those who say the chaplet." Notebook II, 848.

ST. FAUSTINA
Sister, Mystic, "Secretary of Divine Mercy", 1905-1938

"O predestinate souls, slaves of Jesus in Mary, learn that the Hail Mary is the most beautiful of all prayers after the Our Father. It is the most perfect compliment which you can give to Mary, because it is the compliment which the Most High sent her by an archangel in order to win her heart; and it was so powerful over her heart by the secret charms of which it is so full, that in spite of her profound humility she gave her consent to the Incarnation of the Word. It is by this compliment also that you will infallibly win her heart, if you say it as you ought."

ST. LOUIS DE MONTFORT
Priest, 1673-1716

"Prayer is the inner bath of love into which the soul plunges itself."

ST. JOHN VIANNEY
Priest, 1786-1859

"Let us never forget that silent prayer is the strongest and surest act in the struggle against evil." *The Power of Silence,* p.152.

CARDINAL ROBERT SARAH

KEYS TO HIS KINGDOM

"I do not tell you to pray in my way, but in that of God. Leave your soul at liberty to receive the divine impressions according to God's pleasure. We should pray according to the dictates of the Holy Spirit."

ST. PAUL OF THE CROSS
Priest, Founder of the Passionists, 1694-1775

"Whether, therefore, we receive what we ask for, or do not receive it, let us still continue steadfast in prayer. For to fail in obtaining the desires of our heart, when God so wills it, is not worse than to receive it; for we know not as He does, what is profitable to us."

"It is possible to offer fervent prayer even while walking in public or strolling alone, or seated in your shop, . . while buying or selling, . . or even while cooking."

ST. JOHN CHRYSOSTOM
Archbishop, Father and Doctor of the Church, 347-407

"But let our speech and petition when we pray be under discipline, observing quietness and modesty. Let us consider that we are standing in God's sight. We must please the divine eyes both with the habit of body and with the measure of voice."

ST. CYPRIAN OF CARTHAGE
Bishop, Martyr, 210-258

PRAYER

"We should have frequent recourse to prayer and persevere a long time in it. God wishes to be solicited. He is not weary of hearing us. The treasure of His graces is infinite. We can do nothing more pleasing to him than to beg incessantly that He bestow them upon us."

ST. JOHN BAPTIST DE LA SALLE
Priest, 1651-1719

"Pray as though everything depended on God. Work as though everything depended on you."

ST. AUGUSTINE
Bishop, Father and Doctor of the Church, 354-430

"Pray with great confidence, with confidence based upon the goodness and infinite generosity of God and upon the promises of Jesus Christ. God is a spring of living water which flows unceasingly into the hearts of those who pray."

ST. LOUIS DE MONTFORT
Priest, 1673-1716

"The great method of prayer is to have none. If in going to prayer one can form in oneself a pure capacity for receiving the spirit of God, that will suffice for all method."

ST. JANE FRANCES DE CHANTEL
Widow, Nun, 1572-1641

KEYS TO HIS KINGDOM

"We must pray without tiring, for the salvation of mankind does not depend on material success; nor on sciences that cloud the intellect. Neither does it depend on arms and human industries, but on Jesus alone."

ST. FRANCES XAVIER CABRINI
Nun, First U.S. citizen to be canonized, 1850-1917

"For me prayer is a surge of the heart, it is a simple look towards Heaven, it is a cry of recognition and of love, embracing both trial and joy."

ST. THERESE OF LISIEUX
Nun, Doctor of the Church, 1873-1897

"Just as love and self-control destroy evil thought, so contemplation and prayer destroy all self-exaltation."

ST. THALASSIOS THE LIBYAN
Priest, Abott, Fifth Century

"My daughter, those words of your heart are pleasing to Me, and by saying the chaplet you are bringing humankind closer to Me." Notebook II, 929.

ST. FAUSTINA
Sister, Mystic, "Secretary of Divine Mercy", 1905-1938

"Prayer is the encounter of God's thirst with ours."

ST. AUGUSTINE
Bishop, Father and Doctor of the Church, 354-430

PRAYER

"He who does not pray deprives himself of what is indispensable for life."

PADRE PIO
Stigmatic, Mystic, 1897-1968

"Prayer is still a little known means; however, it is the most effective way to reestablish peace in our souls because it allows us to get ever closer to God's love."

ST. MAXIMILIAN KOLBE
Friar, Martyr, 1894-1941

"Every single grace comes to the soul through prayer."

ST. FAUSTINA
Sister, Mystic, "Secretary of Divine Mercy", 1905-1938

"If you would suffer patiently the adversities and the miseries of this life, be a man of prayer."

ST. BONAVENTURE
Bishop, Doctor of the Church, 1217-1274

"There are three things, my brethren, by which faith stands firm, devotion remains constant, and virtue endures. They are prayer, fasting and mercy."

ST PETER CHRYSOLOGUS
Bishop, "Doctor of Homilies", Doctor of the Church, 380-450

KEYS TO HIS KINGDOM

"Prayer is the light of the soul."

ST. JOHN CHRYSOSTOM
Archbishop, Father and Doctor of the Church, 347-407

"Prayer is true rest."

ST. FRANCES OF ASSISI
Friar, Mystic, Stigmatic, 1181-1226

"Virtues are formed by prayer. Prayer preserves temperance. Prayer suppresses anger. Prayer prevents emotions of pride and envy. Prayer draws into the soul the Holy Spirit and raises man to Heaven."

ST. EPHREM OF SYRIA
Doctor of the Church, Theologian, 306-373

"Man is worth as much as he prays."

ST. LUIGI ORIONE
Priest, 1872-1940

"Thanks to prayer, we can be with God."

ST. GREGORY OF NYSSA

"Those who say they don't have time for prayer, are not lacking time, but love."

POPE ST. JOHN PAUL II
1920-2005

PRAYER

"For whatever the virtue you seek, pray. And pray in this way: by reading in the Book of Life, that is, in the life of the One who is God and man, Jesus Christ."

ST. ANGELA OF FOLIGNO
Widow, Mystic, Franciscan tertiary, 1248-130

"Great is the power of prayer — a queen, as one might say, having free access always to the King, and able to obtain whatever she asks."

ST. THERESE OF LISIEUX
Nun, Doctor of the Church, 1873-1897

"When it is well done, it moves the Divine Heart and makes Him always more inclined to grant our requests."

PADRE PIO
Stigmatic, Mystic, 1897-1968

"Give me a man of prayer and he will be capable of everything. He may say with the apostle, 'I can do all things in him who strengthens me."

ST. VINCENT DE PAUL
Priest, 1581-1660

"Everyone of us needs half an hour of prayer each day, except when we are busy—then we need an hour."

ST. FRANCIS DE SALES
Bishop, Doctor of the Church, 1567-1622

KEYS TO HIS KINGDOM

"There are five excellent qualities which are required in all prayer. A prayer must be confident, ordered, suitable, devout and humble."

"We pray, not that we may change the divine decree, but that we may impetrate that which God has decreed to be fulfilled by our prayers."

ST. THOMAS AQUINAS
Angelic Doctor of the Church, 1225-1274

"We do not know the number of souls that is ours to save through our prayers and sacrifices; therefore, let us always pray for sinners." Divine Mercy in my Soul (1783).

ST. FAUSTINA
Sister, Mystic, "Secretary of Divine Mercy", 1905-1938

Chapter 11

Fasting and Mortification

"When you fast, do not look gloomy like the hypocrites. They neglect their appearance, so that they may appear to others to be fasting. Amen, I say to you, they have received their reward. But when you fast, anoint your head and wash your face, so that you may not appear to others to be fasting, except to your Father who is hidden. And your Father who sees what is hidden will repay you.

Matthew 6: 16-18

Fasting and mortification is very important in growing your spiritual life. Scripture teaches us about fasting in both the Old and the New Testament. In the above quote from Matthew, Jesus tells us; "When you fast," He does not say when you decide to fast, so as followers of Jesus we must fast.

In the early Church, fasting was considered an essential part of the faith. In the past century, we have seen the Church water down the requirements to fast and it appears that most Christians now totally disregard even these requirements. Just ask your neighbors, when was the last time they fasted.

We also learn from the blessed how important mortification is for growing in the spiritual life. We learn from exorcists that daily mortifications are one of the best tools in fighting off demonic attacks.

****

"The more one mortifies his natural inclinations, the more he renders himself capable of receiving divine inspirations and of progressing in virtue."

ST. FRANCIS DE SALES
Bishop, Doctor of the Church, 1567-1622

"He who wishes to find Jesus should seek Him, not in the delights and pleasures of the world, but in mortification of the senses."

"St. John of the Cross says that he who teaches that exterior mortification is not necessary is not to be believed, although he should perform miracles."

ST. ALPHONSUS LIGUORI
Bishop, Doctor of the Church, 1696-1787

FASTING AND MORTIFICATION

"Be as eager to break your own will as the thirsty stag is to drink of the refreshing waters."

ST. PAUL OF THE CROSS
Priest, Founder of the Passionists, 1694-1775

"Without mortification nothing can be done."

ST. PHILIP NERI
Priest, "Second Apostle of Rome", 1515-1595

"If any man will come after me, let him deny himself and take up his cross, and follow me." Matthew 16:24.

"Let us read the lives of the saints; let us consider the penances which they performed, and blush to be so effeminate and so fearful of mortifying our flesh."

"My daughter, mortification is like fire which dries up all humors. In the same way, mortification dries up all the bad humors which are present in the soul, and it inundates her with a sanctifying humor, in such a way as to make the most beautiful virtues sprout."

JESUS TO LUISA PICCARRETA

"Where there is no great mortification there is no great sanctity."

ST. PHILIP NERI
Priest, "Second Apostle of Rome", 1515-1595

KEY TO HIS KINGDOM

"There were two saints in the desert, who had sewed thorns into all their clothes; and we seek for nothing but comfort!"

ST. JOHN VIANNEY
Priest, 1786-1859

"He who wishes to find Jesus should seek Him, not in the delights and pleasures of the world, but in mortification of the senses."

"Mortification is of two kinds: interior and exterior. By interior mortification the passions are conquered, and particularly that which prevails over us most. He who does not overcome his predominant passion is in great danger of being lost. On the contrary he who does overcome it, will easily conquer all the rest. Some nevertheless suffer themselves to be swayed by some particular vice, and yet think they are good persons, because they are not overcome by the same vices which they witness in others. "But what will this avail?" says St. Cyril, "a small chink is sufficient to sink the vessel." It avails nought to say: "I cannot abstain from this vice" a resolute will overcomes everything; when it relies on God's assistance which is never wanting.'"

ST. ALPHONSUS LIGUORI
Bishop, Doctor of the Church, 1696-1787

"To do penance is to bewail the evil we have done, and to do no evil to bewail."

POPE ST. GREGORY THE GREAT
Father and Doctor of the Church, 540-604

FASTING AND MORTIFICATION

"Fasting cleanses the soul, raises the mind, subjects one's flesh to the spirit, renders the heart contrite and humble, scatters the clouds of concupiscence, quenches the fire of lust, and kindles the true light of chastity. Enter again into yourself."

ST. AUGUSTINE
Bishop, Father and Doctor of the Church, 354-430

"Mortification must be the breath of the soul. Just as breathing is necessary to the body, and depending on the air it breathes, whether good or bad, it becomes infected or purified - and also, from the breathing it can be known whether the interior of man is healthy or ill, and whether all the vital parts are in harmony - the same for the soul: if she breathes the air of mortification, everything in her will be purified, all of her senses will sound with the same concordant sound; her interior will emit a balsamic, salutary, fortifying breath. If then she does not breathe the air of mortification, everything will be discordant in the soul; she will emit a stinking, disgusting breath; while she is about to tame one passion, another will unbridle... In sum, her life will be nothing but a child's game."

"God hides the prize of eternal glory in our mortification's and in the victory of ourselves, which we always strive for with great gentleness."

ST. JANE FRANCES DE CHANTEL
Widow, Nun, 1572-1641

KEY TO HIS KINGDOM

"I scourge both flesh and spirit because I know that I have offended in both flesh and spirit."

ST. PETER DAMIAN
Monk, Bishop, Doctor of the Church, 1007-1072

"Renounce yourself in order to follow Christ; discipline your body; do not pamper yourself, but love fasting."

ST. BENEDICT OF NURSIA
Monk, 480-547

"There is more security in self-denial, mortification, and other like virtues, than in an abundance of tears."

ST. TERESA OF JESUS
Nun, First women Doctor of the Church, 1515-1582

"Do you fast? Give me proof of it by your works. If you see a poor man, take pity on him. If you see a friend being honored, do not envy him. Do not let only your mouth fast, but also the eye, and the ear, and the feet, and the hands, and all the members of our bodies."

ST. JOHN CHRYSOSTOM
Archbishop, Father and Doctor of the Church, 347-407

"We come to confession quite preoccupied with the shame that we shall feel. We accuse ourselves with hot air. It is said that many confess, and few are converted. I believe it is so, my children, because few confess with tears of repentance. See, the misfortune is, that people

FASTING AND MORTIFICATION

do not reflect. If one said to those who work on Sundays, to a young person who had been dancing for two or three hours, to a man coming out of an alehouse drunk, "What have you been doing? You have been crucifying Our Lord!" they would be quite astonished, because they do not think of it. My children, if we thought of it, we should be seized with horror; it would be impossible for us to do evil. For what has the good God done to us that we should grieve Him thus, and put Him to death again -- Him, who has redeemed us from Hell? It would be well if all sinners, when they are going to their guilty pleasures, could, like St. Peter, meet Our Lord on the way, who would say to them, "I am going to that place where you are going yourself, to be there crucified again." Perhaps that might make them reflect."

ST. JOHN VIANNEY
Priest, 1786-1859

"The Scripture is full of places that prove fasting to be not the invention of man but the institution of God, and to have many more profits than one. And that the fasting of one man may do good unto another, our Saviour showeth himself where he saith that some kind of devils cannot be cast out of one man by another "without prayer and fasting." And therefore, I marvel that they take this way against fasting and other bodily penance."

ST. THOMAS MORE
Martyr, 1478-1535

KEY TO HIS KINGDOM

"The saints understood how great an outrage sin is against God. Some of them passed their lives in weeping for their sins. St. Peter wept all his life; he was still weeping at his death. St. Bernard used to say, "Lord! Lord! it is I who fastened You to the Cross!"

"If you have the courage to imitate Mary Magdalene in her sins, have the courage to imitate her penance!"

PADRE PIO
Stigmatic, Mystic, 1897-1968

"Review, then, in careful thought the innumerable blessings wherewith thy Creator has ennobled thee, no merits of thine own intervening, and call to mind thine own unnumbered evils, thy sole response -- O, how wicked and how undeserved! -- for all those His benefits; and cry out in the pangs of a great grief, "What have I done? Provoked my God, challenged my Creator's anger, repaid Him innumerable ills for untold goods. What have I done?" And speaking thus, rend, rend thy heart, pour forth sighs, weep showers of tears. For if thou weepest not here, when wilt thou weep?"

ST. ANSELM OF CANTERBURY
Monk, Archbishop, Doctor of the Church, 1033-1109

"This morning, I saw my adorable Jesus for just a little, and since obedience had told me to pray for a certain person, when Jesus came I commended her to Him, and He said to Me: 'Humiliation must not only be accepted, but also loved; so much so, as to chew it like food. And just as when a food is bitter, the more one chews it, the

FASTING AND MORTIFICATION

more he feels the bitterness, in the same way, humiliation, when it is well chewed, gives rise to mortification. And these – that is, humiliation and mortification – are two most powerful means in order to get out of certain hitches and obtain those graces which are needed. While it seems to be noxious to the human nature, just like the bitter food which seems to do harm rather than good - so with humility and mortification'."

"But it is not so. The more the piece of iron is beaten on the anvil, the more it sparkles with fire and is purged. The same for the soul: the more she is humiliated and beaten on the anvil of mortification, the more she sparkles with celestial fire and is purged - if she really wants to walk along the path of good. If then she is false, it happens all the opposite." Volume 3, December 30, 1899.

"Mortification is the sight of the soul. As I was in my usual state, my blessed Jesus was delaying in coming. I felt I was dying for the pain of His privation, when, all of a sudden, He came and told me: 'My daughter, just as the eyes are the sight of the body, so mortification is the sight of the soul. Therefore, mortification can be called 'eyes of the soul'." Volume 4, August 5, 1901.

"Mortification produces glory. This morning, I saw my beloved Jesus for just a little, and He seemed to be holding a written paper in His hand, on which one could read: "Mortification produces glory. One who wants to find the fount of all pleasures, must move away from all that may displease God." Having said this, He disappeared. Volume 4, June 17, 1902.

"In addition, the crown of thorns means that there is no glory and honor without thorns; that there can never be dominion over passions and acquisition of virtues without feeling oneself being pricked deep in one's flesh and spirit, and that true reigning is in mastering oneself by the pricks of mortification and of sacrifice." Volume 5, October 12, 1903.

"My daughter, the first bomb which must be primed in the interior of the soul is mortification. When this bomb is thrown into the soul, it knocks everything down and immolates everything to God. In fact, in the soul it is as though there are many palaces, but all of vices, such as pride, disobedience, along with many other vices; and the bomb of mortification, knocking everything down, rebuilds as many other palaces of virtues, immolating them and sacrificing them all to the glory of God." Having said this, He disappeared. *Book of Heaven*, Volume 6, May 28, 1904.

SERVANT OF GOD LUISA PICCARRETTA
Mystic, "Little Daughter of the Divine Will", 1865-1947

"Nothing, how little so ever it be, if it is suffered for God's sake, can pass without merit in the sight of God."

THOMAS A KEMPAS
Priest, 1380-1471

FASTING AND MORTIFICATION

"Fasting is most intimately connected with prayer. For the mind of one who is filled with food and drink is so borne down as not to be able to raise itself to the contemplation of God, or even to understand what prayer means."

CATECHISM OF THE COUNCIL OF TRENT

"Bless those who curse you, and pray for your enemies, and fast for those who persecute you."

DIDACHE

"Fasting is the soul of prayer; mercy is the lifeblood of fasting. So if you pray, fast; if you fast, show mercy; if you want your petition to be heard, hear the petition of others. If you do not close your ear to others, you open God's ear to yourself."

ST PETER CHRYSOLOGUS
Bishop, "Doctor of Homilies", Doctor of the Church, 380-450

"You know that there is no middle course, and that it is a question of being saved or lost for all eternity. It depends on us: either we may choose to love God eternally with the Saints in Heaven after we have done violence to self here below by mortifying and crucifying ourselves as they did, or else renounce their happiness by giving to nature all for which it craves."

ST. MARGARET MARY ALACOQUE
Nun, Mystic, Sacred Heart of Jesus devotion, 1647-1690

KEY TO HIS KINGDOM

"The ultimate goal of fasting is to help each one of us to make a complete gift of self to God."

"Fasting represents an important ascetical practice, a spiritual arm to do battle against every possible disordered attachment to ourselves. Freely chosen detachment from the pleasure of food and other material goods helps the disciple of Christ to control the appetites of nature, weakened by original sin, whose negative effects impact the entire human person."

POPE BENEDICT XVI

"For we fast for three purposes: (1) to restrain the desires of the flesh; (2) to raise the mind to contemplate sublime things; (3) to make satisfaction for our sins. These are good and noble things, and so fasting is virtuous."

ST. THOMAS AQUINAS
Angelic Doctor of the Church, 1225-1274

Chapter 12

Works and Deeds

"For just as a body without a spirit is dead, so also faith without works is dead."

James 2:26

As Catholics we should all know that it is by the grace of God that we are justified (saved). We cannot even pray without the grace of God. Works and deeds do not save us but allow us merit (recompense) from God. The Church teaches us that the merit of man before God arises from the fact that God has freely chosen to associate man with the work of His grace, and that the merits of our good works are gifts of the divine goodness. The more we respond to the grace that God gives us through our works and deeds, the more merit we obtain for Heaven.

****

KEYS TO THE KINGDOM

"Reflect, that the Lord does not only seek flowers, but also fruit; that is, not only good desires and good resolutions, but also good works."

ST. BERNARD OF CLAIRVAUX
Abbot, Doctor of the Church, 1090-1153

"Yes, the first Sunday after Easter is the Feast of Mercy, but there must also be acts of mercy, and I demand the worship of My mercy through the solemn celebration of the Feast and through the veneration of the image which is painted. By means of this image I shall grant many graces to souls. It is to be a reminder of the demands of My mercy, because even the strongest faith is of no avail without works." *Divine Mercy in My Soul,* Notebook 2, (742).

JESUS TO ST. FAUSTINA

"We are not created for this earth. The end for which God has placed us in the world, is this, that by our good works we may merit eternal life. "The end is life everlasting." Romans 6: 22.

"See how a person is justified by works and not by faith alone." James 2:24.

"The proof of love is in the works. Where love exists, it works great things. But when it ceases to act, it ceases to exist."

86

WORKS AND DEEDS

"Man by prayer merits to receive that which God had from all eternity determined to give him."

POPE ST. GREGORY THE GREAT
Father and Doctor of the Church, 540-604

"St. Denis the Areopagite says, "Divine love consists in the affections of the heart more than in the knowledge of the understanding." In human sciences, knowledge excites love; but in the science of the saints, love produces knowledge. He that loves God most, knows him best. Besides, it is not lofty and fruitless conceptions, but works, that unite the soul to God, and make it rich in merits before the Lord."

ST. ALPHONSUS LIGUORI
Bishop, Doctor of the Church, 1696-1787

"By your stubbornness and impenitent heart, you are storing up wrath for yourself for the day of wrath and revelation of the just judgment of God, who will repay everyone according to his works: eternal life to those who seek glory, honor, and immortality through perseverance in good works, but wrath and fury to those who selfishly disobey the truth and obey wickedness." Romans 2; 5-8.

ST. PAUL THE APOSTLE

I heard a voice from heaven say, "Write this: Blessed are the dead who die in the Lord from now on." "Yes," said the Spirit, "let them find rest from their labors, for their works accompany them." Revelation 14:13.

KEYS TO THE KINGDOM

"We have to do the works of the one who sent me while it is still day. Night is coming when no one can work." John 9:4.

"He who is sluggish in prayer, and slothful and negligent in serving his brethren and in performing other holy tasks, is explicitly called an idler by the apostle, and condemned as unworthy even of his bread. For St. Paul writes that the idler is not to have any food (cf. 2 Thess. 3:10); and elsewhere it is said that God hates idlers, that the idle man cannot be trusted, and that idleness has taught great evil (cf. Ecclus. 33:27). Thus, each of us should bear the fruit of some action performed in God's name, even if he has employed himself diligently in but one good work. Otherwise he will be totally barren, and without any share in eternal blessings."

ST. SYMEON METAPHRASTES
Monk, Greek writer, 900- after 984

"Labor the more, that by good works you may make your calling and election sure." 2 Peter 1: 10.

"In the eyes of the sovereign Judge the merit of our actions depends on the motives which prompted them."

POPE ST. GREGORY THE GREAT
Father and Doctor of the Church, 540-604

"I understand that, each time we contemplate with desire and devotion the Host in which is hidden Christ's

WORKS AND DEEDS

Eucharistic Body, we increase our merits in heaven and secure special joys to be ours later in the beatific vision of God."

ST. GERTRUDE THE GREAT
Nun, Mystic, 1256-1302

"Love ought to manifest itself in deeds rather than in words.... love consists in a mutual sharing of goods, for example, the lover gives and shares with the beloved what he possesses, or something of that which he has or is able to give; and vice versa, the beloved shares with the lover. Hence, if one has knowledge, he shares it with the one who does not possess it; and so also if one has honors, or riches. Thus, one always gives to the other. "

ST. IGNATIUS OF LOYOLA
Priest, Mystic, Founder of the Jesuits, 1491-1556

"Let us also love our neighbors as ourselves. Let us have charity and humility. Let us give alms because these cleanse our souls from the stains of sin. Men lose all the material things they leave behind them in this world, but they carry with them the reward of their charity and the alms they give. For these they will receive from the Lord the reward and recompense they deserve."

ST. FRANCES OF ASSISI
Friar, Mystic, Stigmatic, 1181-1226

"Jesus Christ cursed the unfruitful fig tree (Matt. 21:19), and pronounced sentence against the useless servant who had not made any profit on his talent. (Matt. 25:24-

KEYS TO THE KINGDOM

30). All this proves to us that Jesus Christ wishes to receive some fruits from our wretched selves, namely our good works, because those works belong to Him alone: "Created in good works, in Christ Jesus" (Eph. 2:10)—which words of the Holy Spirit show that Jesus Christ is the sole beginning, and ought to be the sole end, of all our good works, and also that we ought to serve Him, not as servants for wages, but as slaves of love." *True Devotion to Mary* p. 43.

ST. LOUIS DE MONTFORT
Priest, 1673-1716

"My children, how sad it is! when a soul is in a state of sin, it may die in that state; and even now, whatever it can do is without merit before God."

ST. JOHN VIANNEY
Priest, 1786-1859

"The majority of souls appear before the Judgment empty-handed. They did nothing good for eternity."

VEN. MARY OF AGREDA
Nun, Abbess, Mystic, 1602-1665

"Our works are of no value if they be not united to the merits of Jesus Christ."

ST. TERESA OF JESUS
Nun, First women Doctor of the Church, 1515-1582

WORKS AND DEEDS

"I would not wish to see one meritorious act attributed to myself, even if it were the means of ensuring my salvation; for I should be worse than a demon, to wish to rob God of his own. Yet it is needful that we ourselves act, for the divine grace neither vivifies nor aids that which does not work itself, and grace will not save us without our cooperation. I repeat it; all works, without the help of grace are dead, being produced by the creature only; but grace aids all works performed by those who are not in mortal sin, and makes them worthy of heaven; not those which are ours solely, but those in which grace cooperates."

ST. CATHERINE OF GENOA
Lay person, Mystic, 1447-1510

"Raphael the angel also witnesses the like, and exhorts that alms should be freely and liberally bestowed, saying, "Prayer is good, with fasting and alms; because alms doth deliver from death, and it purgeth away sins."

"He shows that our prayers and fastings are of less avail, unless they are aided by almsgiving; that entreaties alone are of little force to obtain what they seek, unless they be made sufficient by the addition of deeds and good works. The angel reveals, and manifests, and certifies that our petitions become efficacious by almsgiving, that life is redeemed from dangers by almsgiving, that souls are delivered from death by almsgiving."

ST. CYPRIAN OF CARTHAGE
Bishop, Martyr, 210-258

Chapter 13

The Sacrifice of the Holy Mass

*Then he took a cup, gave thanks, and said, "Take this and share it among yourselves; for I tell you [that] from this time on I shall not drink of the fruit of the vine until the kingdom of God comes." Then he took the bread, said the blessing, broke it, and gave it to them, saying, "This is my body, which will be given for you; **do this in memory of me.**" And likewise the cup after they had eaten, saying, "This cup is the new covenant in my blood, which will be shed for you."*

Luke 22: 17-20

If people truly understood what the Mass was, the churches would be filled to their capacity. Due to the lack of good catechesis, most Catholics do not understand what takes place at the Mass. The Mass is the eternal sacrifice of the Lamb of God. It is the re-presentation of the sacrifice of Jesus on Calvary which makes present His sacrifice of the Cross. There was only one eternal sacrifice by Jesus which he gave us in the Mass so that we may enter into it again and again and be present at it. The Catechism teaches us: When the Church celebrates the Eucharist, she commemorates Christ's Passover, and it is made present: the sacrifice Christ offered once for all on the cross remains ever present. "As often as the sacrifice of the Cross by which 'Christ our Pasch has been sacrificed' is celebrated on the altar, the work of our redemption is carried out." (CCC 1364).

****

"Sunday is the property of our good God; it is His own day, the Lord's Day. He made all the days of the week: He might have kept them all; He has given you six, and has reserved only the seventh for Himself. What right have you to meddle with what does not belong to you? You know very well that stolen goods never bring any profit. Nor will the day that you steal from Our Lord profit you either. I know two very certain ways of becoming poor: they are working on Sunday and taking other people's property."

ST. JOHN VIANNEY
Priest, 1786-1859

"Hear Mass daily; it will prosper the whole day. All your duties will be performed the better for it, and your soul will be stronger to bear its daily cross. The Mass is the most holy act of religion; you can do nothing that can give greater glory to God or be more profitable for your

THE SACRIFICE OF THE HOLY MASS

soul than to hear Mass both frequently and devoutly. It
is the favorite devotion of the saints."

ST. PETER JULIAN EYMARD
Priest, "The Apostle of the Eucharist", 1811-1868

"The Infinite Mass causes the whole heavenly court to
rejoice. It alleviates the pain of the souls in purgatory. It
draws down all types of blessings upon earth, and gives
more glory to God than all the sufferings of all the
martyrs together, more glory than the penances of all the
saints, than all the tears shed by them since the
beginning of the world and all that they may do till the
end of time."

ST. JOHN VIANNEY
Priest, 1786-1859

"The celebration of Holy Mass is as valuable as the death
of Jesus on the cross."

ST. THOMAS AQUINAS
Angelic Doctor of the Church, 1225-1274

"When the Mass is being celebrated, the sanctuary is
filled with countless angels, who adore the Divine Victim
immolated on the altar."

ST. JOHN CHRYSOSTOM
Archbishop, Father and Doctor of the Church, 347-407

KEYS TO THE KINGDOM

"The Mass is infinite like Jesus. . .Ask an angel what the Mass is, and he will reply to you in truth," I understand what it is and why it is offered, but I do not, however, understand how much value it has." One angel, a thousand angels, all of Heaven know this and think like this."

"If we only knew how God regards this Sacrifice, we would risk our lives to be present at a single Mass."

"The earth could exist more easily without the sun than without the Holy Sacrifice of the Mass."

PADRE PIO
Stigmatic, Mystic, 1897-1968

"He who devoutly hears holy Mass will receive a great vigor to enable him to resist mortal sin, and there shall be pardoned to him all venial sins which he may have committed up to that hour."

"Let the entire man be seized with fear; let the whole world tremble; let heaven exult when Christ, the Son of the Living God, is on the altar in the hands of the priest. O admirable height and stupendous condescension! O humble sublimity! O sublime humility! that the Lord of the universe, God and the Son of God, so humbles Himself that for our salvation He hides Himself under a morsel of bread."

ST. FRANCES OF ASSISI
Friar, Mystic, Stigmatic, 1181-1226

THE SACRIFICE OF THE HOLY MASS

"Recognize in this bread what hung on the cross, and in this chalice what flowed from His side... whatever was in many and varied ways announced beforehand in the sacrifices of the Old Testament pertains to this one sacrifice which is revealed in the New Testament."

ST. AUGUSTINE
Bishop, Father and Doctor of the Church, 354-430

"I begin each day with holy Mass, receiving Jesus hidden under the appearance of a simple piece of bread. Then I go out into the streets and I find the same Jesus hidden in the dying destitute, the AIDS patients, the lepers, the abandoned children, the hungry, and the homeless. It's the same Jesus."

"Who is Jesus to me? Jesus is the Word made Flesh. Jesus is the Bread of Life. Jesus is the Victim offered for our sins on the cross. Jesus is the sacrifice offered at holy Mass for the sins of the world and for mine. Jesus is the Word - to be spoken. Jesus is the Truth - to be told. Jesus is the Way - to be walked. Jesus is the Light - to be lit. Jesus is the Life - to be lived. Jesus is the Love - to be loved"

MOTHER TERESA
Nun, 1910-1997

I believe that were it not for the Holy Mass, as of this moment the world would be in the abyss."

ST. LEONARD OF PORT MAURICE
Preacher, Ascetic writer, 1676-1751

97

KEYS TO THE KINGDOM

"No human tongue can enumerate the favors that trace back to the Sacrifice of the Mass. The sinner is reconciled with God; the just man becomes more upright; sins are wiped away; vices are uprooted; virtue and merit increase; and the devil's schemes are frustrated."

ST. LAWRENCE JUSTINIAN
Bishop, 1381-1456

"Put all the good works in the world against one Holy Mass; they will be as a grain of sand beside a mountain."

ST. JOHN VIANNEY
Priest, 1786-1859

"The heavens open and multitudes of angels come to assist in the Holy Sacrifice of the Mass."

POPE ST. GREGORY THE GREAT
Father and Doctor of the Church, 540-604

"The Mass is the most perfect form of prayer."

POPE PAUL VI
1897-1978

"My eyes, I have filled with Jesus upon Whom I have fixed them at the Elevation of the Host at Holy Mass and I do not wish to replace Him with any other image."

ST. COLETTE
Nun, Abbess, 1381-1447

THE SACRIFICE OF THE HOLY MASS

"When I immersed myself in prayer and united myself with all the Masses that were being celebrated all over the world at that time, I implored God, for the sake of all these Holy Masses, to have mercy on the world and especially on poor sinners who were dying at that moment. At the same instant, I received an interior answer from God that a thousand souls had received grace through the prayerful mediation I had offered to God. We do not know the number of souls that is ours to save through our prayers and sacrifices; therefore, let us always pray for sinners."

ST. FAUSTINA
Sister, Mystic, "Secretary of Divine Mercy", 1905-1938

"If we but paused for a moment to consider attentively what takes place in this Sacrament, I am sure that the thought of Christ's love for us would transform the coldness of our hearts into a fire of love and gratitude."

ST. ANGELA OF FOLIGNO
Widow, Mystic, Franciscan tertiary, 1248-1309

"If Christ did not want to dismiss the Jews without food in the desert for fear that they would collapse on the way, it was to teach us that it is dangerous to try to get to heaven without the Bread of Heaven."

"Receive Communion often, very often. There you have the sole remedy, if you want to be cured. Jesus has not put this attraction in your heart for nothing."

KEYS TO THE KINGDOM

"Do you realize that Jesus is there in the tabernacle expressly for you – for you alone? He burns with the desire to come into your heart...don't listen to the demon, laugh at him, and go without fear to receive the Jesus of peace and love."

ST. THERESE OF LISIEUX
Nun, Doctor of the Church, 1873-1897

Chapter 14

The Eucharist

"Jesus said to them: Amen, amen, I say to you: unless you eat the flesh of the Son of Man and drink his blood, you do not have life within you."

John 6: 53

The Catholic Church teaches that in the celebration of the Eucharist, through the power of the Holy Spirit and the actions of the priest, the bread and wine become the Body and Blood of Jesus Christ. That the whole glorified Christ is truly present, Body, Blood, Soul, and Divinity under the appearances of bread and wine.

This is what the Church means when she speaks of the "Real Presence" of Christ in the Eucharist. The Church has always believed and taught this.

The Church at the Fourth Lateran Council in 1215 adopted the term *transubstantiation* to affirm that the substance of the bread and wine are changed in the Eucharist into the substance of Christ's Body and Blood, while the appearances of the bread and wine remain the same.

A simple way to explain transubstantiation to a non-Catholic is to say, "The bread and wine become Jesus. After the consecration, bread and wine are not there anymore, and Jesus is present under the appearances of bread and wine."

The Council of Trent in 1651 reaffirmed this tenet of the Church. The Council stated, "If anyone says that in the most holy sacrament of the Eucharist the substance of bread and wine remains together with the body and blood of our Lord Jesus Christ and denies that wonderful and unique change of the whole substance of the bread into his body and of the whole substance of the wine into his blood while only the species of bread and wine remain, a change which the Catholic Church very fittingly calls transubstantiation, let him be anathema." (*Decree on the Sacrament of the Eucharist*, can. 2; DH 1652).

This belief in the real presence is reaffirmed in the New *Catechism of the Catholic Church* of Pope John Paul II released in 1992. It states in section 1413, "By the consecration the transubstantiation of the bread and wine into the Body and Blood of Christ is brought about. Under the consecrated species of bread and wine Christ himself, living and glorious, is present in a true, real, and substantial manner: his Body and his Blood, with his soul and his divinity (cf. Council of Trent: DS 1640; 1651).

EUCHARIST

In 2019, Pew Research did a study about the level of Catholic belief in the real presence of Jesus in the Eucharist. The results of this study give us an indication of how terrible the catechesis of the Catholic faith has been since the reforms of Vatican II. Even though the Real Presences is a Tenet of the Catholic faith, 69% of the self-identified Catholics said they believed that the bread and wine were symbols of the body and blood of Jesus. What was even worse was that 43% of those even believed that that was the teaching of the Church.[1]

This misunderstanding of the real presence shows that these self-identified Catholics do not understand what is actually taking place during Mass and therefore are missing out on the great gifts that our Lord has given us. Let's read what the blessed say about the Eucharist. I'll start with the early church Fathers then finish with the saints and mystics.

****

"I have no taste for corruptible food nor for the pleasures of this life. I desire the bread of God, which is the flesh of Jesus Christ . . . and for drink I desire his blood, which is love incorruptible" *Letter to the Romans* 7:3 (A.D. 110).

"Take note of those who hold heterodox opinions on the grace of Jesus Christ which has come to us, and see how contrary their opinions are to the mind of God. . . . They abstain from the Eucharist and from prayer because they do not confess that the Eucharist is the flesh of our Savior

---

[1] Pew Research, Short Reads, 2019/08/05

KEYS TO HIS KINGDOM

Jesus Christ, flesh which suffered for our sins and which that Father, in his goodness, raised up again. They who deny the gift of God are perishing in their disputes" *Letter to the Smyrnaeans* 6:2–7:1 (A.D. 110).

ST. IGNATIUS OF ANTIOCH
Bishop, Martyr, 35-108

"For not as common bread nor common drink do we receive these; but since Jesus Christ our Savior was made incarnate by the word of God and had both flesh and blood for our salvation, so too, as we have been taught, the food which has been made into the Eucharist by the Eucharistic prayer set down by him, and by the change of which our blood and flesh is nurtured, is both the flesh and the blood of that incarnated Jesus" *First Apology* 66 (A.D. 151).

"If the Lord were from other than the Father, how could he rightly take bread, which is of the same creation as our own, and confess it to be his body and affirm that the mixture in the cup is his blood?" *Against Heresies* 4:33–32 (A.D. 189).

"He has declared the cup, a part of creation, to be his own blood, from which he causes our blood to flow; and the bread, a part of creation, he has established as his own body, from which he gives increase unto our bodies. When, therefore, the mixed cup [wine and water] and the baked bread receives the Word of God and becomes the Eucharist, the body of Christ, and from these the

EUCHARIST

substance of our flesh is increased and supported, how can they say that the flesh is not capable of receiving the gift of God, which is eternal life—flesh which is nourished by the body and blood of the Lord, and is in fact a member of him?" (ibid., 5:2).

IRENAEUS OF LYONS
Bishop, Church Father and Doctor of the Church, 130-202

"'And she [Wisdom] has furnished her table' [Prov. 9:2] . . . refers to his [Christ's] honored and undefiled body and blood, which day by day are administered and offered sacrificially at the spiritual divine table, as a memorial of that first and ever-memorable table of the spiritual divine supper [i.e., the Last Supper]" Fragment from *Commentary on Proverbs* (A.D. 217).

ST. HIPPOLYTUS
Bishop, Martyr, 170-235

"Formerly, in an obscure way, there was manna for food; now, however, in full view, there is the true food, the flesh of the Word of God, as he himself says: 'My flesh is true food, and my blood is true drink' [John 6:55]" *Homilies on Numbers* 7:2 (A.D. 248).

ORIGEN
Church Father, 185-253

"He [Paul] threatens, moreover, the stubborn and forward, and denounces them, saying, 'Whosoever eat the bread or drinks the cup of the Lord unworthily, is guilty of the body and blood of the Lord' [1 Cor. 11:27]. All these warnings being scorned and contemned— [lapsed Christians will often take Communion] before their sin is expiated, before confession has been made of their crime, before their conscience has been purged by sacrifice and by the hand of the priest, before the offense of an angry and threatening Lord has been appeased, [and so] violence is done to his body and blood; and they sin now against their Lord more with their hand and mouth than when they denied their Lord" *The Lapsed* 15–16 (A.D. 251).

ST. CYPRIAN OF CARTHAGE
Bishop, Martyr, 210-258

"After having spoken thus [at the Last Supper], the Lord rose up from the place where he had made the Passover and had given his body as food and his blood as drink, and he went with his disciples to the place where he was to be arrested. But he ate of his own body and drank of his own blood, while he was pondering on the dead. With his own hands the Lord presented his own body to be eaten, and before he was crucified he gave his blood as drink" *Treatises* 12:6, (A.D. 340).

APHRAAHAT THE PERSIAN SAGE
Bishop, Abbot, Church Father, 270-345

"The bread and the wine of the Eucharist before the holy invocation of the adorable Trinity were simple bread and wine, but the invocation having been made, the bread becomes the body of Christ and the wine the blood of Christ" *Catechetical Lectures* 19:7 (A.D. 350).

EUCHARIST

"Do not, therefore, regard the bread and wine as simply that; for they are, according to the Master's declaration, the body and blood of Christ. Even though the senses suggest to you the other, let faith make you firm. Do not judge in this matter by taste, but be fully assured by the faith, not doubting that you have been deemed worthy of the body and blood of Christ. . . . [Since you are] fully convinced that the apparent bread is not bread, even though it is sensible to the taste, but the body of Christ, and that the apparent wine is not wine, even though the taste would have it so, . . . partake of that bread as something spiritual, and put a cheerful face on your soul" (ibid., 22:6, 9).

CYRIL OF JERSUSALEM
Bishop, Father and Doctor of the Church, 315-386

"Perhaps you may be saying, 'I see something else; how can you assure me that I am receiving the body of Christ?' It but remains for us to prove it. And how many are the examples we might use! . . . Christ is in that sacrament, because it is the body of Christ" *The Mysteries* 9:50, 58 (A.D. 390).

ST. AMBROSE
Bishop, Father and Doctor of the Church, 339-397

"When [Christ] gave the bread he did not say, 'This is the symbol of my body,' but, 'This is my body.' In the same way, when he gave the cup of his blood he did not say, 'This is the symbol of my blood,' but, 'This is my blood'; for he wanted us to look upon the [Eucharistic elements] after their reception of grace and the coming of the Holy Spirit not according to their nature, but receive them as they are, the body and blood of our Lord. We ought . . . not regard [the elements] merely as bread and cup, but as the body and blood of the Lord, into which they were transformed by the descent of the Holy Spirit" *Catechetical Homilies* 5:1 (A.D. 405).

THEODORE OF MOPSUESTIA
Bishop, 392-428

"Christ was carried in his own hands when, referring to his own body, he said, 'This is my body' [Matt. 26:26]. For he carried that body in his hands." *Explanations of the Psalms* 33:1:10 (A.D. 405).

"I promised you [new Christians], who have now been baptized, a sermon in which I would explain the sacrament of the Lord's Table. . . . That bread which you see on the altar, having been sanctified by the word of God, is the body of Christ. That chalice, or rather, what is in that chalice, having been sanctified by the word of God, is the blood of Christ" *Sermons* 227 (A.D. 411).

"What you see is the bread and the chalice; that is what your own eyes report to you. But what your faith obliges you to accept is that the bread is the body of Christ and the chalice is the blood of Christ" (ibid., 272).[2]

ST. AUGUSTINE
Bishop, Father and Doctor of the Church, 354-430

---

[2] The following quotes were taken from www.catholic,com/tract/the-real-presence

EUCHARIST

We will necessarily add this also. Proclaiming the death, according to the flesh, of the only-begotten Son of God, that is Jesus Christ, confessing his resurrection from the dead, and his ascension into heaven, we offer the unbloody sacrifice in the churches, and so go on to the mystical thanksgivings, and are sanctified, having received his holy flesh and the precious blood of Christ the Savior of us all. And not as common flesh do we receive it . . . but as truly the life-giving and very flesh of the Word himself." Session 1, *Letter of Cyril to Nestorius* (A.D. 431).

"Eat my flesh,' [Jesus] says, 'and drink my blood.' The Lord supplies us with these intimate nutrients, he delivers over his flesh and pours out his blood, and nothing is lacking for the growth of his children."

ST. CLEMENT OF ALEXANDRIA
Father of the Church, 150-215

"He said: This is my Body; therefore the Eucharist is not the figure of his Body and Blood, as some have said, talking nonsense in their stupid minds, but it is in very truth the Blood and Body of Christ."

ST. MARCARIUS THE GREAT
Monk, Hermit,300-391

"Adoration outside Holy Mass prolongs and intensifies what has taken place in the liturgical celebration and makes a true and profound reception of Christ possible.

KEYS TO HIS KINGDOM

I . . . warmly recommend, to Pastors and to all the faithful, the practice of Eucharistic adoration."

POPE BENEDICT XVI
1927-2022

"Each morning at Holy Mass, the Bread of Life will help the body as well as the soul, if we have faith. If we but touch the hem of His garment...and how much more have we than that! We can find Him, at every moment, on the altar. Be with Him there. Better than all books! Thank the Trinity over and over again for this Gift. Rest in His presence, and my guardian angel will adore Him for me. Silence."

VENERABEL EDEL QUINN
Layperson, Missionary, 1907-1944

"Mass badly celebrated is an enormous evil. Ah! it is not a matter of indifference how it is said! . . . I have had a great vision on the mystery of Holy Mass and I have seen that whatever good has existed since creation is owing to it."

BLESSED ANNE CATHERINE EMMERICH
Canoness, Stigmatic, Mystic, 1774-1821

"Since Christ Himself has said, "This is My Body" who shall dare to doubt that It is His Body?"

CYRIL OF JERSUSALEM
Bishop, Father and Doctor of the Church, 315-386

Chapter 15

One Holy Catholic Church

"For as the body is one, and hath many members, and all the members of that one body, being many, are one body: so also is Christ. For by one Spirit are we all baptized into one body, whether we be Jews or Gentiles, whether we be bond or free; and have been all made to drink into one Spirit."

1 Corinthians 12:12-13

Anyone who has studied the history of early Christianity understand that there is only one Church that Jesus started on earth, and it is the Roman Catholic Church. This is why so many protestant pastors, as they delve into the early writings of the Church Fathers, come to realize that they do not have the fullness of Christ's teachings in their own Christian communities. It is sad to see that there are thousands of protestant churches today all believing that they are being guided by the Holy Spirit. We know that this is not possible for there is only

111

one true church and the rest are heretical and being misled by the father of all lies.

We must pray that the Holy Spirit will enlighten their members to seek the truth. We must tell them to not rely on fallen away Catholics to tell them what the Catholic Church teaches. They do not know or understand the Church's teachings, because if they did, they would have never walk away from the graces that one receives through the sacraments, especially the Eucharist and confession. Instead, they need to pick up a *Catechism of the Catholic Church*, the *Catechism of Pope Pious the X*, or *The Catechism of the Council of Trent* and read and study it to find out what the Church really believes. We owe it to our brothers and sisters in Christ to guide them to the truth.

****

"I am sent to you to confute, not to embrace your heresy. The Catholic religion is the faith of all ages, I fear not death. . . Pardon my enemies, O Lord: blinded by passion they know not what they do. Lord Jesus, have mercy on me. Mary, Mother of God, succor me!"

ST. FIDELIS OF SIGMARINGEN UPON HIS DEATH
Friar, Martyr,1577-1622

"Just as in one man there is one soul and one body, yet many members; even so the Catholic Church is one body, having many members. The soul that quickens this body is the Holy Spirit; and therefore, in the Creed after confessing our belief in the Holy Spirit, we are bid to believe in the Holy Catholic Church."

ONE HOLY CATHOLIC CHURCH

"The true religion has always been one from the beginning and will always be the same."

"Wherever the bishop shall appear, there let the multitude also be; even as, wherever Jesus Christ is, there is the Catholic Church."

ST. IGNATIUS OF ANTIOCH
Bishop, Martyr, 35-108

"He who does not embrace the teaching of the Church does not have the habit of faith."

"There is but one Church in which men find salvation, just as outside the ark of Noah it was not possible for anyone to be saved."

ST. THOMAS AQUINAS
Angelic Doctor of the Church, 1225-1274

"The extremities of the earth, and all in every part of it who purely and rightly confess the Lord look directly towards the most holy Roman Church and its confession and faith, as it were to a sun of unfailing light, awaiting from it the bright radiance of the sacred dogmas of our Fathers according to what the six inspired and holy councils have purely and piously decreed, declaring most expressly the symbol of faith. For from the coming down of the incarnate Word amongst us, all the Churches in every part of the world have held that greatest Church alone as their base and foundation,

KEYS TO HIS KINGDOM

seeing that according to the promise of Christ our Saviour, the gates of hell do never prevail against it, that it has the keys of a right confession and faith in Him, that it opens the true and only religion to such as approach with piety, and shuts up and locks every heretical mouth that speaks injustice against the Most High."

ST. MAXIMOS THE CONFESSOR
Monk, 508-662

"There are not over a 100 people in the U.S. that hate the Catholic Church, there are millions however, who hate what they wrongly believe to be the Catholic Church. Which is, of course, quite a different thing."

SERVANT OF GOD FULTON J. SHEEN
Theologian. Spiritual writer, 1895-1979

"Either Christ has a Church in the world continually and until the end of the world, or else He has a Church sometimes, and sometimes not at all. Could we think that He had a Church while He was here Himself, and perhaps awhile after, but mysteriously none since? . . . No . . . that can in no way be, since He must necessarily still preserve His Church somewhere; otherwise, how could He be with His followers continually until the end of the world?"

ST. THOMAS MORE
Martyr, 1478-1535

ONE HOLY CATHOLIC CHURCH

"I will go peaceably and firmly to the Catholic Church: for if Faith is so important to our salvation, I will seek it where true Faith first began, seek it among those who received it from God Himself."

ST. ELIZABETH ANN SETON
First U.S. born canonized saint, 1774-1821

"There is only one Christian Faith, that is; Catholic."

ST. BRIDGET OF SWEDEN
Mystic, 1303-1373

"He who does not believe according to the tradition of the Catholic Church is an unbeliever."

ST. JOHN DAMASCENE
Priest, Father and Doctor of the Church, 676-749

"But what is also to the point, let us note that the very tradition, teaching, and faith of the Catholic Church from the beginning was preached by the Apostles and preserved by the Fathers. On this the Church was founded; and if anyone departs from this, he neither is, nor any longer ought to be called, a Christian."

ST. ANTHANAIUS
Bishop, Doctor of the Church, *Father of Orthodoxy*, 296-373

"In fact, there is only one true and holy religion, founded and instituted by Christ Our Lord. Mother and Nurse of the virtues, Destroyer of vice, Liberator of souls, Guide true happiness, she is called Catholic, Apostolic, and Roman."

"Neither the true faith nor eternal salvation is to be found outside the Holy Catholic Church."

BLESSED POPE PIUS IX
Longest reigning Pope behind St. Peter, 1792-1878

"We do not innovate anything...How is it that novelties are introduced which were never even thought of by our predecessors?"

ST. AMBROSE
Bishop, Father and Doctor of the Church, 339-397

"Fly to the Catholic Church! Adhere to the only faith which continues to exist from the beginning, that faith which was preached by Paul and is upheld by the Chair of Peter."

ST. HIPPOLYTUS
Bishop, Martyr

"We must mention another fruitful cause of evil by which the Church is afflicted at present, namely: Indifferentism, that vicious manner of thinking which mushrooms on all sides owing to the wiles of malicious men, and which holds that the eternal salvation of the soul can be obtained by the profession of any faith, provided a man's morals be good and decent ... Let them beware who preach that the gates of Heaven are open to

ONE HOLY CATHOLIC CHURCH

every religion! Let them seriously consider the testimony of the Savior that some are against Christ because they they are not with Christ, that they scatter who do not gather with Him, and therefore without doubt they will perish in eternity unless they hold to the Catholic faith and observe it whole and inviolate."

POPE GREGORY XVI
1765-1846

"The Church alone, being the Bride of Christ and having all things in common with her Divine Spouse, is the depository of the truth."

POPE PIUS X
1835-1914

"Heretics think false things about God and call it their faith."

ST. AUGUSTINE
Bishop, Father and Doctor of the Church, 354-430

"If a soul is not clothed with the teachings of the Church, he cannot merit to have Jesus seated in him."

ST. JEROME
Priest, Father and Doctor of the Church, 1347-1420

KEYS TO HIS KINGDOM

"The Church is the Ship outside which it is impossible to understand the Divine Word, for Jesus spoke from the boat to the people gathered on the shore."

ST. HILARY OF POITIERS
Bishop, Father and Doctor of the Church, 310-367

"Those who are seeking the true religion will never find it outside the Catholic Church alone, because, in every other religion, if they trace it up to the author, they will find some impostor whose imagination furnished a mass of sophisms and errors."

"The definitions of the Church are the rules of true faith."

"The Church of the Lord is built upon the rock of the apostles among so many dangers in the world; it therefore remains unmoved. The Church's foundation is unshakable and firm against assaults of the raging sea. Waves lash at the Church but do not shatter it. Although the elements of this world constantly beat upon the Church with crashing sounds, the Church possesses the safest harbor of salvation for all in distress. There is a stream which flows down on God's saints like a torrent. There is also a rushing river giving joy to the heart that is at peace and makes for peace."

ST. AMBROSE
Bishop, Father and Doctor of the Church, 339-397

ONE HOLY CATHOLIC CHURCH

"There is no middle way between Catholicism and Atheism... Hence, Protestants have abandoned themselves to the extreme of Atheism or Materialism, denying every maxim of faith .. .Oh, God! How does it happen that these new masters of faith do not see that being separated from the Catholic Church, and having lost obedience to her, they have also lost the rule of faith, so that at the present time they have no sure rule by which they can ascertain what is of the faith or what is not; thus, they walk in the dark, changing the articles of their belief from day to day ... On the other hand, its constant uniformity of doctrine in the dogmas of faith, from its first foundation by Jesus Christ, demonstrates the truth of the Catholic Church. It has been the same in all ages, so that the truths we believe at the present day were believed in the first ages."

ST. ALPHONSUS LIGUORI
Bishop, Doctor of the Church, 1696-1787

"To you it is given to know the mystery of the kingdom of God, but to those who are outside all things are done in parables." Mark 4:11.

"Keep close to the Catholic Church at all times, for the Church alone can give you true peace, since she alone possesses Jesus, the true Prince of Peace, in the Blessed Sacrament."

PADRE PIO
Stigmatic, Mystic, 1897-1968

KEYS TO HIS KINGDOM

"Actually, only those are to be included as members of the Church who have been baptized and profess the true faith, and who have not been so unfortunate as to separate themselves from the unity of the Body, or been excluded by legitimate authority for grave faults committed. "For in one spirit" says the Apostle, "were we all baptized into one Body, whether Jews or Gentiles, whether bond or free." As therefore in the true Christian community there is only one Body, one Spirit, one Lord, and one Baptism, so there can be only one faith. And therefore, if a man refuse to hear the Church let him be considered - so the Lord commands - as a heathen and a publican. It follows that those who are divided in faith or government cannot be living in the unity of such a Body, nor can they be living the life of its one Divine Spirit." *De Romano Pontifice,* Book II, Chapter 29.

ST. ROBERT BELLARMINE
Cardinal, Archbishop, Doctor of the Church, 1542-1621

"The preaching of the Church truly continues without change and is everywhere the same. It has the testimony of the Prophets and Apostles and all their disciples."

IRENAEUS OF LYONS
Bishop, Church Father and Doctor of the Church, 130-202

Chapter 16

The Blessed Mother

"And the angel being come in, said unto her: Hail,
full of grace (favored one), the lord is with thee:
blessed art thou among women."

Luke 1:28

Why do the followers of Jesus love his mother so? She is the mother of our God, the Ark of the New Covenant and the new Eve. If the Blessed Mother hadn't said yes to the angel, we would not have had her son Jesus. She gave up her own will to live in God's Will. She was immaculately conceived thus she did not suffer with concupiscence. She was a perpetual virgin. This has always been the teaching of the Church. Jesus did not have any biological brothers or sisters. Mary took a vow of virginity when she entered the temple as a child. Even

THE KEYS TO HIS KINGDOM

the early protesters (reformers) Martin Luther, John Calvin and Ulrich Zwingli stood and believed in her perpetual virginity. [3]

The Blessed Mother stood at the foot of the cross with John when all the other apostles were in hiding in fear of their lives. Even though John's real mother was there at the foot of the cross, Jesus gave his mother to John as his and our spiritual mother. She was there at the cenacle when the Holy Spirit descended down on Pentecost. She was there at the beginning of the Church to help guide the apostles.

The Blessed Mother is the Queen of Heaven rising in glory above the angels. Exorcists tell us that no demon can stand the sight of the Blessed Mother. During an exorcism, if the Blessed Mother appears the demons flee.

You can read in history about the lopsided battles which have been won because of the intersession of the Blessed Mother due to the praying of the rosary. Two examples are the Battle of Lepanto in 1571 and the Battle of Vienna in 1687. The Rosary is one of the most powerful weapons that our Lord has given us for spiritual combat. Pray it daily.

****

"We never give more honor to Jesus than when we honor his Mother, and we honor her simply and solely to honor him all the more perfectly. We go to her only as a way leading to the goal we seek - Jesus, her Son."

---

[3] Max Thurian [Protestant], *Mary: Mother of all Christians*, translated by Neville B. Cryer, New York: Herder & Herder, 1963, 77, 197

122

THE BLESSED MOTHER

"The more the Holy Ghost finds Mary, His dear and inseparable spouse, in any soul, the more active and mighty He becomes in producing Jesus Christ in that soul, and that soul in Jesus Christ." *True Devotion To Mary.*

ST. LOUIS DE MONTFORT
Priest, 1673-1716

"A man cannot rise any higher than this. The Immaculate is the highest degree of perfection and sanctity of a creature. No man will ever attain this celestial summit of grace, for the Mother of God is unique. However, he who gives himself without limits to the Immaculate will in a short time attain a very high degree of perfection and procure for God a very great glory." *Let Yourself Be Led by the Immaculate.*

ST. MAXIMILIAN KOLBE
Friar, Martyr, 1894-1941

"After the love which we owe Jesus Christ, we must give the chief place in our heart to the love of His Mother Mary."

ST. ALPHONSUS LIGUORI
Bishop, Doctor of the Church, 1696-1787

"Love of Mary and devotion to her are a sure sign of obtaining eternal salvation."

ST. BERNARD OF CLAIRVAUX
Abbot, Doctor of the Church, 1090-1153

THE KEYS TO HIS KINGDOM

"Not a single soul who has really persevered in her service has ever been damned."

"According to St. Bonaventure, all the angels in heaven unceasingly call out to her: "Holy, holy, holy Mary, Virgin Mother of God." They greet her countless times each day with the angelic greeting, "Hail, Mary", while prostrating themselves before her, begging her as a favor to honor them with one of her requests. According to St. Augustine, even St. Michael, though prince of all the heavenly court, is the most eager of all the angels to honor her and lead others to honor her. At all times he awaits the privilege of going at her word to the aid of one of her servants."

ST. LOUIS DE MONTFORT
Priest, 1673-1716

"Mary having co-operated in our redemption with so much glory to God and so much love for us, Our Lord ordained that no one shall obtain salvation except through her intercession."

ST. ALPHONSUS LIGUORI
Bishop, Doctor of the Church, 1696-1787

"It is impossible to save one's soul without devotion to Mary and without her protection."

ST. ANSELM OF CANTERBURY
Monk, Archbishop, Doctor of the Church, 1033-1109

THE BLESSED MOTHER

"O sinner, be not discouraged, but have recourse to Mary in all you necessities. Call her to your assistance, for such is the divine Will that she should help in every kind of necessity."

ST. BASIL THE GREAT
Father and Doctor of the Church, 330-379

"Mary seeks for those who approach her devoutly and with reverence, for such she loves, nourishes, and adopts as her children."

ST. BONAVENTURE
Bishop, Doctor of the Church, 1217-1274

"It is impossible to be saved without the help of the Most Blessed Virgin, because those who are not saved by the justice of God are saved by the intercession of Mary."

ST. JOHN CHRYSOSTOM
Archbishop, Father and Doctor of the Church, 347-407

"If you love her, she will shower on you many graces in this life, and be an assurance to you of Heaven hereafter."

ST. JOHN BOSCO
Priest, 1815-1888

"I am not only the Queen of Heaven, but also the Mother of Mercy."

OUR LADY TO ST. FAUSTINA

THE KEYS TO HIS KINGDOM

"Hell is not the lot of any true client of Mary for whom she prays even once, and for whom she says to her Son that she wishes him to be saved ... It is sufficient that you desire our salvation, O Mary, and we cannot help but be saved."

ST. ANSELM OF CANTERBURY
Monk, Archbishop, Doctor of the Church, 1033-1109

"Always stay close to this Heavenly Mother, because she is the sea to be crossed to reach the shores of Eternal Splendour."

PADRE PIO
Stigmatic, Mystic, 1897-1968

"When our hands have touched spices, they give fragrance to all they handle. Let us make our prayers pass through the hands of the Blessed Virgin. She will make them fragrant."

ST. JOHN VIANNEY
Priest, 1786-1859

"Prayer is powerful beyond limits when we turn to the Immaculata who is queen even of God's heart."

ST. MAXIMILIAN KOLBE
Friar, Martyr, 1894-1941

THE BLESSED MOTHER

"The servants of Mary are as sure of getting to Paradise as though they were already there."

"Who are they who are saved and who reign in Heaven? Surely those for whom the Queen of Mercy intercedes ... The clients of Mary will necessarily be saved."

ST. ALPHONSUS LIGUORI
Bishop, Doctor of the Church, 1696-1787

"Jesus honored her before all ages, and will honor her for all ages. No one comes to Him, nor even near Him, no one is saved or sanctified, if he too will not honor her. This is the lot of Angels and of men."

"If you are in danger, if your hearts are confused, turn to Mary; she is our comfort, our help; turn towards her and you will be saved."

ST. FRANCES XAVIER CABRINI
Nun, First U.S. citizen to be canonized, 1850-1917

"No one, not even a sinner, who devoutly recommends himself to her shall ever become the prey of Hell."

ST. CATHERINE OF SIENA
Doctor of the Church, Stigmatic, Mystic, 1347-1380

THE KEYS TO HIS KINGDOM

"Men do not fear a powerful hostile army as the powers of hell fear the name and protection of Mary."

ST. BONAVENTURE
Bishop, Doctor of the Church, 1217-1274

"If you invoke the Blessed Virgin when you are tempted, she will come at once to your help, and Satan will leave you."

ST. JOHN VIANNEY
Priest, 1786-1859

"He who is devout to the Virgin Mother will certainly never be lost."

ST. IGNATIUS OF ANTIOCH
Bishop, Martyr, 35-108

"Not one of those who love her can perish; not one of those who try to imitate her can fail to attain eternal salvation."

ST. JEAN EUDES
Priest, 1601-1680

"As mariners are guided into port by the shining of a star, so Christians are guided to heaven by Mary."

ST. THOMAS AQUINAS
Angelic Doctor of the Church, 1225-1274

THE BLESSED MOTHER

"My children, if you desire perseverance, be devout to our Blessed Lady."

ST. PHILIP NERI
Priest, "Second Apostle of Rome", 1515-1595

"No one will ever be the servant of the Son without serving the Mother."

ST. ILDEPHONSUS, BISHOP
Abbot, Archbishop, 607-667

"In trial or difficulty, I have recourse to Mother Mary, whose glance alone is enough to dissipate every fear."

ST. THERESE OF LISIEUX
Nun, Doctor of the Church, 1873-1897

"Never be afraid of loving the Blessed Virgin Mary too much. You can never love her more than Jesus did. If anyone does not wish to have Mary Immaculate for his mother, he will not have Christ for his brother."

ST. MAXIMILIAN KOLBE
Friar, Martyr, 1894-1941

"The sign of those who will be saved consists in this: that they have a great devotion to Mary in their hearts."

ST. JOHN OF AVILA
Priest, Doctor of the Church, 1500-1569

THE KEYS TO HIS KINGDOM

"Devotion to Mary is a sure sign of predestination to him who possesses it."

BL. ALAN DE LA ROCHE
Dominican Preacher, theologian, 1428-1475

"All the sins of your life seem to be rising up against you. Don't give up hope! On the contrary, call your holy mother Mary, with the faith and abandonment of a child. She will bring peace to your soul."

ST. JOSEMARIA ESCRIVA
Priest, Founder of Opus Dei, 1902-1975

"Mary is the Mysterious Book of Predestination to glory."

ST. FRANCES XAVIER CABRINI
Nun, First U.S. citizen to be canonized, 1850-1917

"Let not that man presumes to look for mercy from God who offends His Holy Mother!"

ST. LOUIS DE MONTFORT
Priest, 1673-1716

"Let us run to Mary, and, as her little children, cast ourselves into her arms with a perfect confidence."

ST. FRANCIS DE SALES
Bishop, Doctor of the Church, 1567-1622

THE BLESSED MOTHER

"May I give you some advice for you to put into practice daily? When your heart makes you feel those low cravings, say slowly to the Immaculate Virgin: Look on me with compassion. Don't abandon me. Don't abandon me, my Mother! -- And recommend this prayer to others."

ST. JOSEMARIA ESCRIVA
Priest, Founder of Opus Dei, 1902-1975

"Not only do they offend thee, O Lady, who outrage thee, but thou art also offended by those who neglect to ask thy favors . . . He who neglects the service of the Blessed Virgin will die in his sins . . . He who does not invoke thee, O Lady, will never get to Heaven . . . Not only will those from whom Mary turns her countenance not be saved, but there will be no hope of their salvation . . . No one can be saved without the protection of Mary."

ST. BONAVENTURE
Bishop, Doctor of the Church, 1217-1274

"I therefore command all my Brothers, those living now and those to come in the future, to venerate the Holy Mother of God, whom we always implore to be our Protectress, to praise her at all times, in all circumstances of life, with all the means in their power and with the greatest devotion and submission."

ST. FRANCES OF ASSISI
Friar, Mystic, Stigmatic, 1181-1226

THE KEYS TO HIS KINGDOM

"She is the eldest daughter of the Great King. If you enjoy her favor, she will introduce you to the Monarch of the Universe. No one has so great an interest with Him than Mary, who was the occasion of His coming down from Heaven to become man for the redemption of mankind."

ST. JOHN THE ALMONER
Patriarch of Alexandria, 552-616

"Oh, how I love my Mother! She knows it; and then Jesus Himself gave Her to me, and told me to love Her very much. And what great kindness this Heavenly Mother has always shown me! What would have become of me, if I have not had Her? She has always helped me in my spiritual wants; She has preserved me from countless dangers; She has freed me from the hands of the devil who was ceaselessly coming to attack me; She pleaded my cause with Jesus when I sinned, and She soothed Him when I moved Him to anger by my wicked life; She has taught me to know Him and to love Him, to be good and to please Him. Ah, my dear Mother, I will love Thee always and forever!"

ST. GEMMA GALGANI
Mystic, Stigmatic, 1878-1903

"The Holy Rosary is the best artillery against demons and their followers."

ST. DOMINIC
Founder of the Dominicans, 1170-1221

THE BLESSED MOTHER

"In the Heavens Mary commands the angels and the blessed. As a recompense for her profound humility, God has empowered her and commissioned her to fill with saints the empty thrones from which the apostate angels fell by pride." *Speculum B. V.*, lect. XI. no. 6.

ST. BONAVENTURE
Bishop, Doctor of the Church, 1217-1274

"When Mary holds you up, you do not fall; when she protects you, you need not fear; when she leads you, you do not tire; when she is favorable to you, you arrive at the harbor of safety."

ST. BERNARD OF CLAIRVAUX
Abbot, Doctor of the Church, 1090-1153

"To be devout to you, O holy Virgin, is an arm of salvation which God gives to those whom he wishes to save."

ST. JOHN DAMASCENE
Priest, Father and Doctor of the Church, 676-749

Prayers to the Blessed Mother

Hail Mary

Hail Mary full of grace, the Lord is with thee.
Blessed art thou among women, and blessed is the fruit of thy womb, Jesus.
Holy Mary Mother of God, pray for us sinners, now and at the hour of our death. Amen.

133

THE KEYS TO HIS KINGDOM

Memorare

REMEMBER, O most gracious Virgin Mary, that never was it known that anyone who fled to thy protection, implored thy help, or sought thy intercession was left unaided. Inspired with this confidence, I fly to thee, O Virgin of virgins, my Mother; to thee do I come; before thee I stand, sinful and sorrowful. O Mother of the Word Incarnate, despise not my petitions, but in thy mercy hear and answer me. Amen.

Hail Holy Queen

Hail, Holy Queen, Mother of Mercy, our life, our
sweetness and our hope.
To thee do we cry, poor banished children of Eve.
To thee do we send up our sighs,
mourning and weeping in this valley of tears.
Turn then, most gracious advocate,
thine eyes of mercy toward us, and after this our exile
show unto us the blessed fruit of thy womb, Jesus.
O clement, O loving,
O sweet Virgin Mary. Amen.

Chapter 17

Heaven

"Then I saw a new heaven and a new earth; the first Heaven and the first earth had disappeared now, and there was no longer any sea. I saw the holy city, the new Jerusalem, coming down out of heaven from God, prepared as a bride dressed for her husband. Then I heard a loud voice call from the throne, 'Look, here God lives among human beings. He will make his home among them; they will be his people, and he will be their God, God-with-them. He will wipe away all tears from their eyes; there will be no more death, and no more mourning or sadness or pain. The world of the past has gone."

Revelations 21:1-4

KEYS TO HIS KINGDOM

"The Church teaches us that Heaven is the ultimate end and fulfillment of the deepest human longings, the state of supreme, definitive happiness." (CCC 1024). It also teaches us that "Heaven is the blessed community of all who are perfectly incorporated into Christ." (CCC 1026). Heaven is what we were created for to spend our eternal life with God.

****

"Today I was in heaven, in spirit, and I saw its unconceivable beauties and the happiness that awaits us after death. I saw how all creatures give ceaseless praise and glory to God. I saw how great is happiness in God, which spreads to all creatures, making them happy; and then all the glory and praise which springs from this happiness returns to its source; and they enter into the depths of God, contemplating the inner life of God, the Father, the Son, and the Holy Spirit, whom they will never comprehend or fathom. This source of happiness is unchanging in its essence, but it is always new, gushing forth happiness for all creatures." *Divine Mercy in My Soul,* Notebook II, (777).

ST. FAUSTINA
Sister, Mystic, "Secretary of Divine Mercy", 1905-1938

"No one will have any other desire in heaven than what God wills; and the desire of one will be the desire of all; and the desire of all and of each one will also be the desire of God."

ST. ANSELM OF CANTERBURY
Monk, Archbishop, Doctor of the Church, 1033-1109

HEAVEN

"At present we have a human body but in the future we will have a celestial one, because there are human bodies and celestial bodies. There is a human splendor and a celestial splendor. The splendor that can be attained on earth is temporary and limited, while that of heaven last forever, which will be shown when the corruptible becomes incorruptible and the mortal immortal."

ST. BASIL THE GREAT
Father and Doctor of the Church, 330-379

"If you knew what sweetness awaits the souls of the just in heaven, you would be resolved to endure all the sorrows, persecutions, and insults in this passing life with gratitude. Even if your very cell was full of worms and they gnawed on your flesh throughout your entire life, you would accept it all in order not to lose that heavenly joy which God has prepared for those who love him."

"If the Apostle Paul himself was unable to describe heavenly glory and joy, what other tongue could describe the beauty of the heavenly abode which the souls of the just inhabit? I cannot tell you of the heavenly joy and sweetness I experienced there."

ST. SERAPHIM OF SAROV
Priest, Mystic, 1754-1833

"Earth hath no sorrow that heaven cannot heal."

ST. THOMAS MORE
Martyr, 1478-1535

KEYS TO HIS KINGDOM

St. Anna Schäffer describes what she saw on her three-day visit to heaven: "While I was praying, I was enraptured from the world. My life was hanging by a thread. The clouds opened up and a marvelous garden full of flowers appeared in which I could walk a long distance."

"I cannot describe to you all of the marvels that our good God gives to those He loves... "Yes, there are also meadows and forests, rivers and mountains, homes and buildings, but everything is transparent and spiritualized, while here on earth everything is tainted."

ST. ANNA SCHAFFER
Lay person, Mystic, Stigmatic, 1882-1925

"O my dear parishioners, let us endeavor to get to heaven! There we shall see God. How happy we shall feel! If the parish is converted, we shall go there in procession with the parish priest at the head. ... We must get to heaven!"

ST. JOHN VIANNEY
Priest, 1786-1859

"My crown in heaven should shine with innocence and its flowers should be radiant as the sun. Sacrifices are the flowers Jesus and Mary chose."

ST. BERNADETTE SOUBIROUS
Blessed Mother appeared to her at Lourdes, 1844-1879

HEAVEN

"The Saints stand around my Son like countless stars, whose glory is not to be compared with any temporal light. Believe me, if the Saints could be seen shining with the glory they now possess, no human eye could endure their light all would turn away, dazzled and blinded."

BLESSED MOTHER TO ST. BRIDGET

"Thou wilt see the incomparable beauty of the Angels, for it is believed that those celestial spirits will assume bodies of great loveliness formed from the air, in order to render themselves visible to the blessed. This opinion is held by St. Anselm. And if the beauty of an Angel immeasurably exceeds all human beauty, wilt thou not rejoice in the contemplation of so many thousands of Angelic beings, all of surpassing loveliness, for all eternity?" *The Last Four Things.*

FATHER MARTIN VON COCHEM
Theologian, 1625-1712

"A precious crown is reserved in Heaven for those who perform all their actions with all the diligence of which they are capable; for it is not sufficient to do our part well, it must be done more than well."

"He who beholds Heaven with a pure eye, sees better the darkness of earth; for, although the latter seems to have some brilliancy, it disappears before the splendor of the heavens."

ST. IGNATIUS OF LOYOLA
Priest, Mystic, Founder of the Jesuits, 1491-1556

KEYS TO HIS KINGDOM

"Know that on account of the inexpressible charity that the blessed have towards one another, that each takes no less pleasure in the exaltation of another than if it were his own. Nay, more, he who is greater wishes that the lower were equal to him, and even more honored than himself; for in his triumph he, too, would triumph." *The Last Four Things* p. 146.

ST. JOHN THE BAPTIST
IN A VISION TO ST. AUGUSTINE

"Let us think, if we only got to heaven, what a sweet and easy thing it will be there to be always saying with the angels and the saints, Sanctus, Sanctus, Sanctus."

ST. PHILIP NERI
Priest, "Second Apostle of Rome", 1515-1595

"The path to Heaven is narrow, rough and full of wearisome and trying ascents, nor can it be trodden without great toil; and therefore wrong is their way, gross their error, and assured their ruin who, after the testimony of so many thousands of saints, will not learn where to settle their footing."

ST. ROBERT SOUTHWELL
Priest, Martyr, 1561-1595

Chapter 18

Purgatory, The Final Purification of The Elect

"Settle with your opponent quickly while on the way to court with him. Otherwise your opponent will hand you over to the judge, and the judge will hand you over to the guard, and you will be thrown into prison. Amen, I say to you, you will not be released until you have paid the last penny."

Matthew 5:25-26

If it wasn't for God's merciful gift of Purgatory most souls would end up in Hell. You must understand that nothing unclean can enter Heaven. Scripture teaches us, "but nothing unclean will enter it, nor any[one] who does abominable things or tells lies." (Rev: 21:27). We must be purified of any punishment due to our sins that we have not paid our debt for by a cleansing or purifying fire before we can enter into Heaven. The Church calls this final purification Purgatory.

****

"He then took up a collection among all his soldiers, amounting to two thousand silver drachmas, which he sent to Jerusalem to provide for an expiatory sacrifice. In doing this he acted in a very excellent and noble way, inasmuch as he had the resurrection in mind; for if he were not expecting the fallen to rise again, it would have been superfluous and foolish to pray for the dead. But if he did this with a view to the splendid reward that awaits those who had gone to rest in godliness, it was a holy and pious thought. Thus he made atonement for the dead that they might be absolved from their sin." 2 Maccabees 12: 43-46.

"'He is there,' said her angel, 'and he suffers much. Would you be willing to endure some pain in order to diminish his?' 'Certainly,' she replied, 'I am ready to suffer anything to assist him.' Instantly her angel conducted her into a place of frightful torture. 'Is this, then, hell, my brother?' asked the holy maiden, seized with horror. 'No, sister,' answered the angel, 'but this part of purgatory is bordering upon hell.'

"Looking around on all sides, she saw what resembled an immense prison surrounded with walls of a prodigious height, the blackness of which, together with the monstrous stones, inspired her with horror. Approaching this dismal enclosure, she heard a confused noise of lamenting voices, cries of fury, chains, instruments of torture, violent blows which the executioners discharged upon their victims. This noise was such that all the tumult of the world, in tempest or battle, could bear no comparison to it. 'What, then, is that horrible place?' asked St. Lidwina of her good angel. 'Do you wish me to show it to you?' 'No, I beseech you,' said she, recoiling with terror, 'the noise I hear is so frightful that I can no longer bear it; how, then, could I endure the sight of those horrors?'

"Continuing her mysterious route, she saw an angel seated sadly on the curb of a well. 'Who is that angel?' she asked of her guide. 'It is,' he replied, 'the angel-guardian of the sinner in whose lot you are interested. His soul is in this well, where it has a special purgatory.'

"At these words Lidwina cast an inquiring glance at her angel; she desired to see that soul which was dear to her, and endeavored to release it from that frightful pit. Her angel, who understood her, having taken off the cover of the well, a cloud of flames, together with the most plaintive cries, came forth." Do you recognize that voice?' said the angel to her. 'Alas! yes,' answered the servant of God. 'Do you desire to see that soul?' he continued. On her replying in the affirmative, he called him by his name; and immediately our virgin saw appear at the mouth of the pit a spirit all on fire, resembling incandescent metal, which said to her in a voice scarcely audible, 'O Lidwina, servant of God, who will give me to contemplate the face of the Most High?'

"The sight of this soul, a prey to the most terrible torment of fire, gave our saint such a shock that the cincture which she wore around her body was rent in twain; and, no longer able to endure the sight, she awoke suddenly from her ecstasy. The persons present, perceiving her fear, asked her its cause. 'Alas!" she replied, 'how frightful are the prisons of Purgatory! It was to assist the souls that I consented to descend thither. Without this motive, if the whole world were given to me, I would not undergo the terror which that horrible spectacle inspired.'

"Some days later, the same angel whom she had seen so dejected appeared to her with a joyful countenance; he told her that the soul of his protégé had left the pit and passed into the ordinary purgatory. This partial alleviation did not suffice the charity of Lidwina; she continued to pray for the poor patient, and to apply to him the merits of her sufferings, until she saw the gates of heaven opened to him." *Purgatory,* Chapter 7, p.23-24, by Fr. F. X. Schouppe.

ST. LIDWINA OF SCHIEDAM
Lay person, Mystic, 1380-1433

"It is definite that only a few chosen ones do not go to Purgatory and the sufferings there that one must endure exceed our imagination."

"No tongue can tell nor explain, no mind understand, the grievousness of purgatory. But I, though I see that there is in purgatory as much pain as in hell, yet see the soul which has the least stain of imperfection accepting purgatory, as I have said, as though it were a mercy, and holding its pain of no account as compared with the least stain which hinders a soul in its love. "I seem to see that

THE FINAL PURIFICATION OF THE ELECT

the pain which souls in purgatory endure because of whatever in them displeases God, that is what they have willfully done against his so great goodness, is greater than any other pain they feel in purgatory. And this is because, being in grace, they see the truth and the grievousness of the hindrance which stays them from drawing near to God." *Treatise on Purgatory.*

ST. CATHERINE OF GENOA
Lay person, Mystic, 1447-1510

"The fire of Purgatory is the same as the fire of Hell; the difference between them is that the fire of Purgatory is not everlasting."

ST. JOHN VIANNEY
Priest, 1786-1859

"Let us help and commemorate them. If Job's sons were purified by their father's sacrifice [Job 1:5], why would we doubt that our offerings for the dead bring them some consolation? Let us not hesitate to help those who have died and to offer our prayers for them."

ST. JOHN CHRYSOSTOM
Archbishop, Father and Doctor of the Church, 347-407

"I am the Mother of all the Poor Souls, for my prayers serve to mitigate their sufferings every single hour that they remain there (purgatory)."

OUR BLESSED MOTHER TO ST. BRIDGET

THE KEYS TO HIS KINGDOM

"I saw my guardian angel, who ordered me to follow him. In a moment I was in a misty place full of fire in which there was a great crowd of suffering souls. They were praying fervently, but to no avail, for themselves; only we can come to their aid. The flames, which were burning them, did not touch me at all. My guardian angel did not leave me for an instant. I asked these souls what their greatest suffering was. They answered me in one voice that their greatest torment was longing for God. "I saw Our Lady visiting the souls in purgatory. The souls call her 'The Star of the Sea.' She brings them refreshment. I wanted to talk with them some more, but my guardian   angel beckoned me to leave. We went out of that prison of suffering. [I heard an interior voice, which said] 'My mercy does not want this, but justice demands it. Since that time I am in closer communion with the suffering souls.'" *Divine Mercy in My Soul.*

ST. FAUSTINA
Sister, Mystic, "Secretary of Divine Mercy", 1905-1938

"And one who has recognized My Will and has submitted himself to It, not in everything and always, but in great part, has formed so many paths and receives so much, that Purgatory sends him quickly to Heaven." *Book of Heaven*, Volume 20. November 4, 1926.

JESUS TO LUISA PICCARRETA

"If during life, we have been kind to the suffering souls in purgatory, God will see that help be not denied us after death."

ST. PAUL OF THE CROSS
Priest, Founder of the Passionists, 1694-1775

THE FINAL PURIFICATION OF THE ELECT

"Temporal punishments are suffered by some in this life only, by some after death, by some both here and hereafter, but all of them before that last and strictest judgment. But not all who suffer temporal punishments after death will come to eternal punishments, which are to follow after that judgment."

ST. AUGUSTINE
Bishop, Father and Doctor of the Church, 354-430

"The clients of this most merciful Mother are very fortunate. She helps them both in this life and in the next, consoling them and sponsoring their cause in Purgatory. For the simple reason that the Souls in Purgatory need help so desperately, since they cannot help themselves, our Mother of Mercy does so much more to relieve them. She exercises over these Poor Souls, who are the spouses of Christ, particular dominion, with power to relieve them and even deliver them from their pains. See how important it is then to have devotion to this good Lady, because she never forgets her servants as long as they suffer in these flames. If she helps all the Poor Souls, she is especially indulgent and consoling to her own clients." *The Glories of Mary.*

"The practice of recommending to God the souls in Purgatory, that He may mitigate the great pains which they suffer, and that He may soon bring them to His glory, is most pleasing to the Lord and most profitable to us. For these blessed souls are His eternal spouses, and most grateful are they to those who obtain their deliverance from prison, or even a mitigation of their torments. When, therefore, they arrive in Heaven, they will be sure to remember all who have prayed for them."

"By assisting them we shall not only give great pleasure to God, but will acquire also great merit for ourselves. And, in return for our suffrages, these blessed souls will not neglect to obtain for us many graces from God, but particularly the grace of eternal life. I hold for certain that a soul delivered from Purgatory by the suffrages of a Christian, when she enters paradise, will not fail to say to God: "Lord, do not suffer to be lost that person who has liberated me from the prison of Purgatory, and has brought me to the enjoyment of Thy glory sooner than I have deserved."

ST. ALPHONSUS LIGUORI
Bishop, Doctor of the Church, 1696-1787

"The more one longs for a thing, the more painful does deprivation of it become. And because after this life, the desire for God, the Supreme Good, is intense in the souls of the just (because this impetus toward Him is not hampered by the weight of the body, and that time of enjoyment of the Perfect Good would have come) had there been no obstacle; the soul suffers enormously from the delay."

ST. THOMAS AQUINAS
Angelic Doctor of the Church, 1225-1274

"As we enter Heaven, we will see them, so many of them, coming towards us and thanking us. We will ask who

THE FINAL PURIFICATION OF THE ELECT

they are, and they will say 'a poor soul you prayed for in purgatory."

VENERABLE BISHOP FULTON SHEEN
Theologian, Spiritual writer, 1895-1979

"I do not think that apart from the felicity of Heaven, there can be a joy comparable to that experienced by the souls in Purgatory. An incessant communication from God renders their joy more vivid from day to day: and this communication becomes more and more intimate, to the extent that it consumes the obstacles still existing in the soul... On the other hand, they endure pain so intense, that no tongue is able to describe it. Nor is any mind capable of comprehending the smallest spark of that consuming fire, unless God should show it to him by a special grace."

ST. CATHERINE OF SIENA
Doctor of the Church, Stigmatic, Mystic, 1347-1380

"I come to tell you that they suffer in Purgatory, that they weep, and that they demand with urgent cries the help of your prayers and your good works. I seem to hear them crying from the depths of those fires which devour them: 'Tell our loved ones, tell our children, tell all our relatives how great the evils are which they are making us suffer. We throw ourselves at their feet to implore the help of their prayers. Ah! Tell them that since we have been separated from them, we have been here burning in the flames!'"

THE KEYS TO HIS KINGDOM

"If it were but known how great is the power of the good souls in Purgatory with the Heart of God, and if we knew all the graces we can obtain through their intercession, they would not be so much forgotten. We must, therefore, pray much for them, that they may pray much for us."

ST. JOHN VIANNEY
Priest, 1786-1859

"My love urges Me to release the poor souls. If a beneficent king leaves his guilty friend in prison for justice's sake, he awaits with longing for one of his nobles to plead for the prisoner and to offer something for his release. Then the king joyfully sets him free. Similarly, I accept with highest pleasure what is offered to Me for the poor souls, for I long inexpressibly to have near Me those for whom I paid so great a price. By the prayers of thy loving soul, I am induced to free a prisoner from purgatory as often as thou dost move thy tongue to utter a word of prayer!"

JESUS TO ST. GERTRUDE

"No one is barred from heaven. Whoever wants to enter heaven may do so because God is merciful. Our Lord will welcome us into glory with His arms wide open. The Almighty is pure however, and if a person is conscious of the least trace of imperfection and at the same time understands that Purgatory is ordained to do away with such impediments, the soul enters this place of perfection gladly to accept so great a mercy of God. The worst suffering of these suffering souls is to have sinned against Divine Goodness and not to have been purified in this life."

ST. CATHERINE OF GENOA
Lay person, Mystic, 1447-1510

"Even more since she has given all of herself to Me in life, it is justice that I give all of myself to her at her death. Admitting her to the beatific vision without delay. So, if one gives herself completely to Me, the flames of Purgatory has nothing to do with her." *Book of Heaven*, Volume 5, July 7, 1903.

JESUS TO LUISA PICCARRETA

Prayer for the Souls in Purgatory

"Eternal Father, I offer you the most precious blood of your divine son Jesus in union with the masses said throughout the world today for all the holy souls in purgatory, for sinners everywhere, sinners in the universal church, those in my own home and within my family. Amen, Jesus, Jesus, Jesus". *St. Gertrude*

Chapter 19

Hell

*"And these shall go into everlasting punishment:
but the just into life everlasting."*

Matthew 25:46

It is our decision to choose now whether we want to spend eternity in Heaven or Hell. By our life choices, we decide our fate. God has revealed to us through his Son, Scripture, and His Church what he demands from us. It is up to us if we choose to believe and accept it or not. For instance, the Church teaches that it is a mortal sin to purposely miss Mass on Sunday and left unrepented will send you to Hell. Your excuse might be that you stayed out late the night before and would rather sleep in. You think to yourself it is no big deal, but it is. God gave us the third commandment; "Remember the sabbath and keep it holy." So, by purposely not going to Mass you have broken the third commandment. Now you must look at the first commandment which is: "I am the Lord thy God: thou shalt not have strange gods before me." Your telling God that sleeping in is more important to you than going to Mass. In essences, you have made sleeping in a false God. Through your actions, you are telling God that you know what is more important than he does. This is such an insult to God.

****

"Today, I was led by an Angel to the chasms of hell. It is a place of great torture; how awesomely large and extensive it is! The kinds of tortures I saw: the first torture that constitutes hell is the loss of God; the second is perpetual remorse of conscience; the third is that one's condition will never change; the fourth is the fire that will penetrate the soul without destroying it-a terrible suffering, since it is a purely spiritual fire, lit by God's anger; the fifth torture is continual darkness and a terrible suffocating smell, and, despite the darkness, the devils and the souls of the damned see each other and all the evil, both of others and their own; the sixth torture is the constant company of Satan; the seventh torture is horrible despair, hatred of God, vile words, curses and blasphemies.

"These are the tortures suffered by all the damned together, but that is not the end of the sufferings. There are special tortures destined for particular souls. These are the torments of the senses. Each soul undergoes terrible and indescribable sufferings, related to the manner in which it has sinned. There are caverns and pits of torture where one form of agony differs from

HELL

another. I would have died at the very sight of these tortures if the omnipotence of God had not supported me. Let the sinner know that he will be tortured throughout all eternity, in those senses which he made use of to sin. I am writing this at the command of God, so that no soul may find an excuse by saying there is no hell, or that nobody has ever been there, and so no one can say what it is like.

"I, Sister Faustina, by the order of God, have visited the abysses of hell so that I might tell souls about it and testify to its existence. I cannot speak about it now; but I have received a command from God to leave it in writing. The devils were full of hatred for me, but they had to obey me at the command of God. What I have written is but a pale shadow of the things I saw. But I noticed one thing: that most of the souls there are those who disbelieved that there is a hell. When I came to, I could hardly recover from the fright. How terribly souls suffer there! Consequently, I pray even more fervently for the conversion of sinners. I incessantly plead God's mercy upon them. O my Jesus, I would rather be in agony until the end of the world, amidst the greatest sufferings, than offend You by the least sin." *Divine Mercy in My Soul*, Notebook II, (741).

ST. FAUSTINA
Sister, Mystic, "Secretary of Divine Mercy", 1905-1938

"A long time after the Lord had already granted me many of the favors I've mentioned and other very lofty ones, while I was in prayer one day, I suddenly found that, without knowing how, I had seemingly been put in hell.

KEYS TO HIS KINGDOM

"I understood that the Lord wanted me to see the place the devils had prepared there for me and which I merited because of my sins. This experience took place within the shortest space of time, but even were I to live for many years I think it would be impossible for me to forget it.

"The entrance it seems to me was similar to a very long and narrow alleyway, like an oven, low and dark and confined; the floor seemed to me to consist of dirty, muddy water emitting foul stench and swarming with putrid vermin. At the end of the alleyway a hole that looked like a small cupboard was hollowed out in the wall; there I found I was placed in a cramped condition. All of this was delightful to see in comparison with what I felt there. What I have described can hardly be exaggerated.

"But as to what I then felt, I do not know where to begin if I were to describe it; it is utterly inexplicable. I felt a fire in my soul but such that I am still unable to describe it. My bodily sufferings were unendurable. I have undergone most painful sufferings in this life, and, as the physicians say, the greatest that can be borne, such as the contraction of my sinews when I was paralyzed, without speaking of other ills of different types - yet, even those of which I have spoken, inflicted on me by Satan; yet all these were as nothing in comparison with what I then felt, especially when I saw that there would be no intermission nor any end to them.

"These sufferings were nothing in comparison with the anguish of my soul, a sense of oppression, of stifling, and of pain so acute, accompanied by so hopeless and cruel an infliction, that I know not how to speak of it. If I say that the soul is continually being torn from the body it would be nothing for that implies the destruction of life by the hands of another, but here it is the soul itself that is tearing itself in pieces. I cannot describe that inward fire or that despair, surpassing all torments and all pain. I did not see who it was that tormented me, but I felt myself on fire, and torn to pieces, as it seemed to me; and I repeat it, this inward fire and despair are the greatest torments of all.

"Left in that pestilential place, and utterly without the power to hope for comfort, I could neither sit nor lie down; there was no room. I was placed as it were in a hole in the wall; and those walls, terrible to look on of themselves, hemmed me in on every side. I could not breathe. There was no light, but all was thick darkness. I do not understand how it is; though there was no light, yet everything that can give pain by being seen was visible.

"Our Lord at that time would not let me see more of Hell. Afterwards I had another most fearful vision, in which I saw the punishment of certain sins. They were the most horrible to look at, but because I felt none of the pain, my terror was not so great. In the former vision Our Lord made me really feel those torments and that anguish of spirit, just as if I had been suffering them in the body there. I know not how it was, but I understood distinctly that it was a great mercy that Our Lord would have me see with my own eyes the very place from which His compassion saved me. I have listened to people speaking of these things and I have at other times dwelt on the various torments of Hell, though not often, because my soul made no progress by the way of fear; and I have read of the diverse tortures, and how the devils tear the flesh with red-hot pincers. But all is as nothing before this: It is a wholly different matter. In short, the one is a reality, the other a description; and all burning here in this life is as nothing compared with the fire that is there.

"I was so terrified by that vision, and that terror is on me even now as I write, that though it took place nearly six years ago, the natural warmth of my body is chilled by fear even now when I think of it. And so, amid all the pain and suffering which I may have had to bear, I remember no time in which I do not think that all we have to suffer in this world is as nothing. It seems to me that we complain without reason. I repeat it, this vision was one of the grandest mercies of God."

ST. TERESA OF AVILA
Nun, First women Doctor of the Church, 1515-1582

"My soul fell into abysmal depths, the bottom of which cannot be seen, for it is immense. . . ; Then I was pushed into one of those fiery cavities and pressed, as it were, between burning planks, and sharp nails and red-hot irons seemed to be piercing my flesh. I felt as if they were endeavoring to pull out my tongue, but could not. This torture reduced me to such agony that my very eyes seemed to be starting out of their sockets. I think this was because of the fire which burns, burns. . . not a finger nail escapes terrifying torments, and all the time one cannot move even a finger to gain some relief, not change posture, for the body seems flattened out and [yet] doubled in two. Sounds of confusion and blasphemy cease not for an instant. A sickening stench asphyxiates and corrupts everything, it is like the burning of

HELL

putrefied flesh, mingled with tar and sulfur. . . a mixture to which nothing on earth can be compared. . . although these tortures were terrific, they would be bearable if the soul were at peace. But it suffers indescribably. . . All I have written," she concluded, "is but a shadow of what the soul suffers, for no words can express such dire torment." (September 4, 1922) *Way of Divine Life.*

SISTER JOSEFA MENENDEZ
Nun, Mystic, 1890-1923

"Hell is full of good wishes and desires."

ST. BERNARD OF CLAIRVAUX
Abbot, Doctor of the Church, 1090-1153

"To form a better idea of their lamentable fate, let us imagine a town where the Cains and Neros and all the other wicked men who have defiled the earth—men whom human justice gets rid of by casting them into dungeons and convict prisons—were put together. Let us further suppose that in this town there were no police or military to prevent these wretches from killing and tearing one and another apart. Well, that would be hell such as it is described by the prophet Job: "a land...where no order, but everlasting horror dwells."

"Such is the punishment of damnation. Having lost God, the damned have thereby lost all hope, all dignity, and all consolation." *The End of The Present World*, p.188.

FATHER CHARLES ARMINJON
Priest, 1824-1885

KEYS TO HIS KINGDOM

"Hell is a prison that will also serve as an abode for the rebellious angels and for the demons; this abode cannot be other than the most unpleasant, obscure, and ignominious of all created; it is fitting that it should be at opposite ends and at the greatest distance from the one destined for the elect. Now, the elect will reign eternally in the highest part of heaven, which is the empyrean heaven, and so the lowest part of the earth is the place will the damned will suffer their eternal torments."

FRANCISCO SUAREZ
Jesuit, Philosopher, Theologian, Doctor Eximius, 1548-1617

Chapter 20

Confession

*"Whose sins you forgive are forgiven them,
whose sins you retain are retained".*

John 20:23

Confession is one of the greatest graces that God has given us, yet so few Catholics take advantage of it. I believe that the reason many people refuse to go to confession is due to the sin of pride. If you want to obtain salvation you must humble yourself before God. Going to confession regularly makes you examine your faults and shortcomings which helps you to better understand how to correct your sinful habits. It eases your conscious and reunites your relationship with God.

****

KEYS TO HIS KINGDOM

"You shall judge righteously. You shall not make a schism, but you shall pacify those that contend by bringing them together. You shall confess your sins. You shall not go to prayer with an evil conscience. This is the way of light" (Letter of Barnabas 19 [A.D. 74]).

ST. BARNABAS
Apostle, Bishop, Church Father

"[The bishop conducting the ordination of the new bishop shall pray:] God and Father of our Lord Jesus Christ. . . . Pour forth now that power which comes from you, from your royal Spirit, which you gave to your beloved Son, Jesus Christ, and which he bestowed upon his holy apostles . . . and grant this your servant, whom you have chosen for the episcopate, [the power] to feed your holy flock and to serve without blame as your high priest, ministering night and day to propitiate unceasingly before your face and to offer to you the gifts of your holy Church, and by the Spirit of the high priesthood to have the authority to forgive sins, in accord with your command" (Apostolic Tradition 3 [A.D. 215]).

ST. HIPPOLYTUS
Bishop, Martyr

"Let us not listen to those who deny that the Church of God has the power to forgive all sins."

ST. AUGUSTINE
Bishop, Father and Doctor of the Church, 354-430

CONFESSION

"Good Christians make an examination of conscience and an act of contrition every evening. There was a devout monk lying at the point of death; when his Superior came and told him to make his confession, he answered: "Blessed be God! I have for thirty years made an examination of conscience every evening, and have made my confession every day as if I were at the point of death."

"The devil does not bring sinners to hell with their eyes open: he first blinds them with the malice of their own sins. Before we fall into sin, the enemy labors to blind us, that we may not see the evil we do and the ruin we bring upon ourselves by offending God. After we commit sin, he seeks to make us dumb, that, through shame, we may conceal our guilt in confession."

ST. ALPHONSUS LIGUORI
Bishop, Doctor of the Church, 1696-1787

"Confession is an act of honesty and courage - an act of entrusting ourselves, beyond sin, to the mercy of a loving and forgiving God."

POPE ST. JOHN PAUL II
1920-2005

"My daughter, just as you prepare in My presence, so also you make your confession before Me. The person of the priest is, for Me, only a screen. Never analyze what sort of a priest it is that I am making use of; open your soul in confession as you would to Me, and I will fill it with My light." Notebook VI, (1725).

KEYS TO HIS KINGDOM

"Daughter, when you go to confession, to this fountain of My mercy, the Blood and Water which came forth from My Heart always flows down upon your soul and ennobles it. Every time you go to confession, immerse yourself in My mercy, with great trust, so that I may pour the bounty of My grace upon your soul. When you approach the confessional, know this, that I Myself am waiting there for you. I am only hidden by the priest, but I myself act in your soul. Here the misery of the soul meets the God of mercy. Tell souls that from this fount of mercy souls draw graces solely with the vessel of trust. If their trust is great, there is no limit to My generosity. The torrents of grace inundate humble souls. The proud remain always in poverty and misery, because My grace turns away from them to humble souls." *Divine Mercy in My Soul.*

ST. FAUSTINA
Sister, Mystic, "Secretary of Divine Mercy", 1905-1938

"The confession of evil works is the first beginning of good works."

"If you excuse yourself in confession, you shut up sin within your soul, and shut out pardon."

ST. AUGUSTINE
Bishop, Father and Doctor of the Church, 354-430

"Go to your confessor; open your heart to him; display to him all the recesses of your soul; take the advice that he will give you with the utmost humility and simplicity.

CONFESSION

For God, Who has an infinite love for obedience, frequently renders profitable the counsels we take from others, but especially from those who are the guides of our souls."

"Confession and contrition are so beautiful and fragrant that they erase the ugliness and dissipate the stench of sin."

ST. FRANCIS DE SALES
Bishop, Doctor of the Church, 1567-1622

"In the life of the body a man is sometimes sick, and unless he takes medicine, he will die. Even so in the spiritual life a man is sick on account of sin. For that reason, he needs medicine so that he may be restored to health; and this grace is bestowed in the Sacrament of Penance."

ST. THOMAS AQUINAS
Angelic Doctor of the Church, 1225-1274

"Strive always to confess your sins with a deep knowledge of your own wretchedness and with clarity and purity."

ST. JOHN OF THE CROSS
Priest, Mystic, Doctor of the Church, 1542-1591

"To do penance is to bewail the evil we have done, and to do no evil to bewail."

POPE ST. GREGORY THE GREAT
Father and Doctor of the Church, 540-604

KEYS TO HIS KINGDOM

"We come to confession quite preoccupied with the shame that we shall feel. We accuse ourselves with hot air. It is said that many confess, and few are converted. I believe it is so, my children, because few confess with tears of repentance. See, the misfortune is, that people do not reflect. If one said to those who work on "Sundays, to a young person who had been dancing for two or three hours, to a man coming out of an alehouse drunk, "What have you been doing? You have been crucifying Our Lord!" they would be quite astonished, because they do not think of it. My children, if we thought of it, we should be seized with horror; it would be impossible for us to do evil. For what has the good God done to us that we should grieve Him thus, and put Him to death again -- Him, who has redeemed us from Hell? It would be well if all sinners, when they are going to their guilty pleasures, could, like St. Peter, meet Our Lord on the way, who would say to them, "I am going to that place where you are going yourself, to be there crucified again." Perhaps that might make them reflect."

"The good God knows everything, even before you confess it to him, he already knows that you will sin again and, nevertheless, he forgives you. How great is the love of our God that leads him even to voluntarily forget the future in order to forgive us!"

ST. JOHN VIANNEY
Priest, 1786-1859

"The Blessed Evangelist Matthew tells us, that this man was not alone dumb but blind also. And blind is every man who follows not after that Light Which says: I am

CONFESSION

the Light of the world; he that followeth Me walketh not in darkness, but shall have the Light of life (Jn. 8:12). And he is indeed dumb who confesses not his sins, and who knows not how to open his mouth to the praise of God."

ST. BRUNO
Priest, 1030-1101

"The want of proper examination, true contrition, and a firm purpose of amendment, is the cause of bad confessions, and of the ruin of souls."

ST. BENEDICT JOSEPH LABRE
Layman, Franciscan Tertiary, 1748-1783

"If the poor world could see the beauty of the sinless soul, all sinners, all unbelievers would be instantly converted."

PADRE PIO
Stigmatic, Mystic, 1897-1968

"Never let yourselves be deceived by the devil by keeping silent about some sin in confession out of shame. I assure you, beloved young people, that my hand trembles as I write these lines at the mere thought that a great number of Christians are eternally lost because they have not sincerely declared their sins in confession."

ST. JOHN BOSCO
Priest, 1815-1888

KEYS TO HIS KINGDOM

"God makes no distinction; He promised mercy to all and granted His priests the authority to forgive without any exception."

ST. AMBROSE
Bishop, Father and Doctor of the Church, 339-397

"Just as the man baptized by the priest is enlightened by the Grace of the Holy Spirit, so he who in penance confesses his sins, receives through the priest forgiveness by virtue of the grace of Christ."

ST. ANTHANAIUS
Bishop, Doctor of the Church, *Father of Orthodoxy*, 296-373

"Before going to confession, it is good to ask God for the good will to be holy."

ST. PHILIP NERI
Priest, "Second Apostle of Rome", 1515-1595

Act of Contrition

O my God, I am heartily sorry for having offended Thee, and I detest these and all my sins because I dread the lost of Heaven and pains of hell, but most of all because they offend Thee, my God, who art all good and deserving of all my love. I firmly resolve with the help of Thy grace to sin no more and to avoid the near occasion of sin. Amen.

Chapter 21

Mercy

"Praise the Lord for He is good;

for his mercy endures forever;"

Psalm 136:1

The omnipotent God, who is the creator of all things, sending His only Son to die for our redemption is the greatest sign of mercy in the history of mankind. What greater mercy can there be?

When meditating on God's mercy one must remember that there are two kinds of mercy: mercy that is shown by God to man, and mercy shown by man to others. While we're still here on earth, we should take advantage of all the graces that God offers us through His Church and His sacraments. Do not wait. Now is the time to ask for His mercy. You do not know when your death will come.

KEYS TO HIS KINGDOM

It is also very important that we show mercy to others. In our dealings with our neighbors and family members, regardless of how we feel toward them, we must show them the same mercy that God has shown us.

Remember that when we pray the *Our Father,* we are asking God to; "forgive us are trespasses as we forgive those who trespass against us..." so if we are not merciful towards others, He will not be merciful towards us.

****

"For there are three ways of performing an act of mercy: the merciful word, by forgiving and by comforting; secondly, if you can offer no word, then pray - that too is mercy; and thirdly, deeds of mercy. And when the Last Day comes, we shall be judged from this, and on this basis we shall receive the eternal verdict." Notebook III, (1158).

"Let souls who are striving for perfection particularly adore My mercy, because the abundance of graces which I grant them flows from My mercy. I desire that these souls distinguish themselves by boundless trust in My mercy. I myself will attend to the sanctification of such souls. I will provide them with everything they will need to attain sanctity." *Divine Mercy in My Soul,* Notebook V, (1578).

ST. FAUSTINA
Sister, Mystic, "Secretary of Divine Mercy", 1905-1938

MERCY

"Extend your mercy towards others, so that there can be no one in need whom you meet without helping. For what hope is there for us if God should withdraw His Mercy from us?"

ST. VINCENT DE PAUL
Priest, 1581-1660

"The saints are like the stars. In his providence Christ conceals them in a hidden place that they may not shine before others when they might wish to do so. Yet they are always ready to exchange the quiet of contemplation for the works of mercy as soon as they perceive in their heart the invitation of Christ."

ST. ANTHONY OF PADUA
Priest, Doctor of the Church, 1195-1231

"I have opened My Heart as a living fountain of mercy. Let all souls draw life from it. Let them approach this sea of mercy with great trust. Sinners will attain justification, and the just will be confirmed in good. Whoever places his trust in My Mercy will be filled with My divine peace at the hour of death." Notebook V, (1520).

"The graces of my mercy are drawn by means of one vessel only, and that is – Trust. The more a soul trusts, the more it will receive." Notebook V (1578).

"Before I come as a just Judge, I first open wide the door of My mercy. He who refuses to pass through the door of My mercy must pass through the door of My Justice." Notebook V, (1146).

KEYS TO HIS KINGDOM

"Today I am sending you with My mercy to the people of the whole world. I do not want to punish aching mankind, but I desire to heal it, pressing it to My Merciful Heart. I use punishment when they themselves force Me to do so; My hand is reluctant to take hold of the sword of justice. Before the Day of Justice I am sending the Day of Mercy." Notebook V. (1588).

"I remind you, My daughter, that as often as you hear the clock strike the third hour, immerse yourself completely in My mercy, adoring and glorifying it; invoke its omnipotence for the whole world, and particularly for poor sinners; for at that moment mercy was opened wide for every soul. In this hour you can obtain everything for yourself and for others for the asking; it was the hour of grace for the whole world-mercy triumphed over justice." Notebook V, (1572).

"I am love and Mercy Itself. There is no misery that could be a match for My mercy, neither will misery exhaust it, because as it is being granted – it increases. The soul that trusts in My mercy is most fortunate, because I Myself take care of it." *Divine Mercy in My Soul*, Notebook IV, 1273.

JESUS TO ST. FAUSTINA

"Let no one mourn that he has fallen again and again; for forgiveness has risen from the grave."

ST. JOHN CHRYSOSTOM
Archbishop, Father and Doctor of the Church, 347-407

MERCY

"Those who sincerely say 'Jesus, I trust in You' will find comfort in all their anxieties and fears. There is nothing that man needs more than Divine Mercy — that love which is benevolent, which is compassionate, which raises man above his weakness to the infinite heights of the holiness of God."

ST. JOHN PAUL I
1912-1978

"Apart from the mercy of God, there is no other source of hope for mankind."

POPE ST. JOHN PAUL II
1920-2005

"Father of mercy and God of all consolation, graciously look upon me and impart to me the blessing which flows from this holy Sacrament. Overshadow me with Your loving kindness and let this divine Mystery bear fruit in me."

ST. BLAISE
Bishop, Martyr, -316

"It is not God that acts like an enemy, but you; that is, God does not refuse to make peace with sinners, but they are unwilling to be reconciled with him."

"The judge may be appeased before judgment, but not during judgment." says St. Augustine. Let us, then, with St. Bernard, say to the Lord: "I desire to present myself before Thee already judged, and not to be judged." My

KEYS TO HIS KINGDOM

Judge, I desire to be judged and punished by Thee in life, now that it is the time for mercy, and that Thou canst pardon me; for after death it will be the time for justice."

"If we should be saved and become saints, we ought always to stand at the gates of the Divine mercy to beg and pray for, as alms, all that we need."

ST. ALPHONSUS LIGUORI
Bishop, Doctor of the Church, 1696-1787

"Jesus affirms that mercy is not only an action of the Father, it becomes a criterion for ascertaining who his true children are. In short, we are called to show mercy because mercy has first been shown to us. Pardoning offenses becomes the clearest expression of merciful love, and for us Christians it is an imperative from which we cannot excuse ourselves. At times how hard it seems to forgive! And yet pardon is the instrument placed into our fragile hands to attain serenity of heart. To let go of anger, wrath, violence, and revenge are necessary conditions to living joyfully. Let us therefore heed the Apostle's exhortation: "Do not let the sun go down on your anger" (Eph 4:26). Above all, let us listen to the words of Jesus who made mercy an ideal of life and a criterion for the credibility of our faith: "Blessed are the merciful, for they shall obtain mercy." (Mt 5:7)..." *Misericordiae Vultus*.

POPE BENEDICT XVI
1927-2022

MERCY

"No one is strong in his own strength, but he is safe by the grace and mercy of God."

ST. CYPRIAN OF CARTHAGE
Bishop, Martyr, 210-258

"Place your hopes in the mercy of God and the merits of our Redeemer; say often, looking at the crucifix: There are centered all my hopes."

ST. PAUL OF THE CROSS
Priest, Founder of the Passionists, 1694-1775

"I feel a great desire to abandon myself with greater trust to the Divine Mercy and to place my hope in God alone."

PADRE PIO
Stigmatic, Mystic, 1897-1968

"No just man suffices unto himself for the winning of justification. The divine mercy must always hold out a hand to his footsteps as they falter and almost stumble, and this is so because the weakness of his free will may cause him to lose balance, and if he falls he may perish forever."

"... there is clearly expressed for us what it is we must attribute either to free will or to the decision and daily assistance of the Lord. We are characterized by whether we respond zealously or lackadaisically to the kindly dispensations of God. This perspective is plainly expressed in the healing of the two blind men. Jesus was

175

passing by, a fact made possible by God's provident grace. And the achievement of their own faith and belief was to cry out 'Lord, son of David, have mercy on us' (Mt. 20:31). The restored sight of their eyes is the gift of divine mercy."

"The thief who received the kingdom of heaven, though not as the reward of virtue, is a true witness to the fact that salvation is ours through the grace and mercy of God."

ST. JOHN CASSIAN
Monk, Mystic writer, Church Father, 360-435

Prayer for Mercy

Divine Mercy Chaplet

Use a rosary to recite this chaplet.

Make the Sign of the Cross.

Start by repeating three times: O Blood and Water, which gushed forth from the Heart of Jesus as a fount of mercy for us, I trust in You!

Our Father..., Hail Mary..., The Apostles Creed

The Apostles Creed: I believe in God, the Father Almighty, Creator of Heaven and earth; and in Jesus Christ, His only Son Our Lord, Who was conceived by the Holy Spirit, born of the Virgin Mary, suffered under

MERCY

Pontius Pilate, was crucified, died, and was buried. He descended into Hell; the third day He rose again from the dead; He ascended into Heaven, and sitteth at the right hand of God, the Father Almighty; from thence He shall come to judge the living and the dead. I believe in the Holy Spirit, the holy Catholic Church, the communion of saints, the forgiveness of sins, the resurrection of the body and life everlasting. Amen.

On the large bead before each decade say:

Eternal Father, I offer You the Body and Blood, Soul and Divinity of Your dearly beloved Son, Our Lord Jesus Christ, in atonement for our sins and those of the whole world.

On the ten small beads of each decade: For the sake of His sorrowful Passion, have mercy on us and on the whole world

After the last decade, say the following prayer three times:

Holy God, Holy Mighty One, Holy Immortal One, have mercy on us and on the whole world.

Optional closing prayer:

Eternal God, in Whom mercy is endless and the treasury of compassion — inexhaustible, look kindly upon us and increase Your mercy in us, that in difficult moments we might not despair nor become despondent, but with great confidence submit ourselves to Your holy will, which is Love and Mercy itself. Amen.

Chapter 22

Suffering

"For the sake of Christ, then, I am content with weaknesses, insults, hardships, persecutions, and calamities; for when I am weak then I am strong."

2 Corinthians 12:7-10

Learning how to suffer is one of the greatest keys to obtaining salvation. One must imitate Christ and pick up their cross. Without the cross there is no salvation. It is only through God's grace that one can be content with suffering. St Paul tells us, we suffer "to make us rely, not on ourselves but on God who raises the dead." (2 Corinthians 1:9) You must teach yourself to unite your suffering with Jesus's suffering and then offer it to God for what intention you would like. For example, you can offer it up as penance for your sins. You can offer it up for the poor souls in Purgatory who are being purified by fire. You can offer it up for the salvation of your family members or dear friends. Jesus revealed to Servant of God Luisa Piccarreta that if you offer it up in His Divine Will it becomes an eternal act of love that never ends.

****

"It is true that in this life even the saints suffer, because this earth is the place of merits. And we cannot merit without suffering; but says St. Bonaventure, Divine love is like honey, which makes the most bitter things sweet and amiable."

ST. ALPHONSUS LIGUORI
Bishop, Doctor of the Church, 1696-1787

"The better thou disposest thyself for suffering, the more wisely dost thou act, and the more dost thou merit: and thou wilt bear it more easily, thy mind being well prepared for it and accustomed to it."

THE IMITATION OF CHRIST

"A quarter of an hour of voluntary pains is enough to make up for and surpass all the most atrocious pains that exist in the world; because these are in the human order, while voluntary ones are in the Divine Order." *Book of Heaven,* Volume 29, April 2, 1931.

SERVANT OF GOD LUISA PICCARRETTA
Mystic, "Little Daughter of the Divine Will", 1865-1947

SUFFERING

"There is but one price at which souls are bought, and that is suffering united to My suffering on the cross. Pure love understands these words; carnal love will never understand them." Notebook 1: (324).

"My daughter, meditate frequently on the sufferings which I have undergone for your sake, and then nothing of what you suffer for Me will seem great to you. You please Me most when you mediate on My Sorrowful Passion. Join your little sufferings to My Sorrowful Passion, so that they may have infinite value before My Majesty." *Divine Mercy in My Soul*, Notebook 5: (1512).

JESUS TO ST. FAUSTINA

"If you really want to love Jesus, first learn to suffer, because suffering teaches you to love."

"It is true Jesus, if I think of what I have gone through as a child and now as a grown-up girl I see that I have always had crosses to bear; But oh! how wrong are those who say that suffering is a misfortune!"

ST. GEMMA GALGANI
Mystic, Stigmatic, 1878-1903

"You will be consoled according to the greatness of your sorrow and affliction; the greater the suffering, the greater will be the reward."

ST. MARY MAGDALEN DE'PAZZI
Nun. Mystic, Uncorrupt, 1566-1607

KEYS TO HIS KINGDOM

"The road is narrow. He who wishes to travel it more easily must cast off all things and use the cross as his cane. In other words, he must be truly resolved to suffer willingly for the love of God in all things."

ST. JOHN OF THE CROSS
Priest, Mystic, Doctor of the Church, 1542-1591

"We always find that those who walked closest to Christ were those who had to bear the greatest trials."

ST. TERESA OF AVILA
Nun, First women Doctor of the Church, 1515-1582

"When it is all over you will not regret having suffered; rather you will regret having suffered so little, and suffered that little so badly."

ST. SABASTIAN VALFRE
Priest, 1629-1710

"It is You Jesus, stretched out on the cross, who gives me strength and are always close to the suffering soul. Creatures will abandon a person in his suffering, but You, O Lord, are faithful." *Divine Mercy in My Soul,* Notebook 5; 1508.

ST. FAUSTINA
Sister, Mystic, "Secretary of Divine Mercy", 1905-1938

SUFFERING

"Nothing afflicts the heart of Jesus so much as to see all His sufferings of no avail to so many."

ST. JOHN VIANNEY
Priest, 1786-1859

"I send sufferings to the creatures, so that they may find Me in the sufferings. I am as though wrapped within those pains, and if the soul suffers with patience, with love, she tears the wrapping that covers Me, and she finds Me. Otherwise, I remain hidden in the pain, she will not have the good of finding Me, and I will not have the good of revealing Myself." *Book of Heaven,* Volume 12, April 6, 1918.

JESUS TO LUISA PICCARRETA

"As iron is fashioned by fire and on the anvil, so in the fire of suffering and under the weight of trials, our souls receive that form which our Lord desires them to have."

ST. MADELINE SOPHIE BARAT
1779-1865

"By suffering we are able to give something to God. The gift of pain, of suffering is a big thing and cannot be accomplished in Paradise."

PADRE PIO
Stigmatic, Mystic, 1897-1968

KEYS TO HIS KINGDOM

"The greatness of our love of God must be tested by the desire we have of suffering for His love."

ST. PHILIP NERI
Priest, "Second Apostle of Rome", 1515-1595

"If God sends you many sufferings, it is a sign that He has great plans for you and certainly wants to make you a saint."

ST. IGNATIUS OF LOYOLA
Priest, Mystic, Founder of the Jesuits, 1491-1556

"All the science of the Saints is included in these two things: To do, and to suffer. And whoever had done these two things best, has made himself most saintly."

ST. FRANCIS DE SALES
Bishop, Doctor of the Church, 1567-1622

"We should strive to keep our hearts open to the sufferings and wretchedness of other people, and pray continually that God may grant us that spirit of compassion which is truly the spirit of God."

ST. VINCENT DE PAUL
Priest, 1581-1660

"God had one son on earth without sin, but never one without suffering."

ST. AUGUSTINE
Bishop, Father and Doctor of the Church, 354-430

SUFFERING

"And the Lord said to me, 'My child, you please Me most by suffering. In your physical as well as your mental sufferings, My daughter, do not seek sympathy from creatures. I want the fragrance of your suffering to be pure and unadulterated. I want you to detach yourself, not only from creatures, but also from yourself...The more you will come to love suffering, My daughter, the purer your love for Me will be.'"

JESUS TO ST. FAUSTINA

"When I shrink from suffering, Jesus reproves me and tells me that He did not refuse to suffer. Then I say 'Jesus, Your will and not mine'. At last, I am convinced that only God can make me happy, and in Him I have placed all my hope..."

ST. GEMMA GALGANI
Mystic, Stigmatic, 1878-1903

"Let us, at any rate, give heed to suffer joyfully the crosses that God sends us, because they all, if we are saved, will become for us eternal joys. When infirmities, pains, or any adversities afflict us, let us lift up our eyes to heaven and say, "One day all these pains will have an end, and after them I hope to enjoy God forever."

ST. ALPHONSUS LIGUORI
Bishop, Doctor of the Church, 1696-1787

KEYS TO HIS KINGDOM

"Without the burden of afflictions, it is impossible to reach the height of grace. The gift of grace increases as the struggle increases."

ST. ROSE OF LIMA
Lay person, 1586-1617

"A cross carried simply, and without those returns of self-love which exaggerate troubles, is no longer a cross. Peaceable suffering is no longer suffering. We complain of suffering! We should have much more reason to complain of not suffering, since nothing makes us more like Our Lord than carrying His Cross. Oh, what a beautiful union of the soul with Our Lord Jesus Christ by the love and the virtue of His Cross!"

"You must either suffer in this life or give up the hope of seeing God in Heaven. Sufferings and persecutions are of the greatest avail to us, because we can find therein a very efficient means to make atonement for our sins, since we are bound to suffer for them either in this world or in the next."

ST. JOHN VIANNEY
Priest, 1786-1859

"He longs to give us a magnificent reward. He knows that suffering is the only means of preparing us to know Him as He knows Himself, and to become ourselves divine."

ST. THERESE OF LISIEUX
Nun, Doctor of the Church, 1873-1897

SUFFERING

"Trials and tribulations offer us a chance to make reparation for our past faults and sins. On such occasions the Lord comes to us like a physician to heal the wounds left by our sins. Tribulation is the divine medicine."

ST. AUGUSTINE
Bishop, Father and Doctor of the Church, 354-430

"I think He intends to try you like gold in the crucible, so as to number you amongst His most faithful servants. Therefore, you must lovingly embrace all occasions of suffering, considering them as precious tokens of His love. To suffer in silence and without complaint is what He asks of you."

ST. MARGARET MARY ALACOQUE
Nun, Mystic, Sacred Heart of Jesus devotion, 1647-1690

"Those who pray and suffer, leaving action for others, will not shine here on earth; but what a radiant crown they will wear in the kingdom of life! Blessed be the 'apostolate of suffering'!"

ST. JOSEMARIA ESCRIVA
Priest, Founder of Opus Dei, 1902-1975

"My life manifests itself in the creatures through words, through works and through sufferings, but what manifests It more clearly are the sufferings." *Book of Heaven*, Volume 6, April 29, 1904.

JESUS TO LUISA PICCARRETA

KEYS TO HIS KINGDOM

"For unto you it is given for Christ, not only to believe in him, but also to suffer for him." Philippians 1: 29.

"Consider it all joy, my brothers, when you encounter various trials, for you know that the testing of your faith produces perseverance." James: 12-3.

Prayers For Suffering

Dear Lord,
Help me to remember in these troubled times
The cross you carried for my sake,
So that I may better carry mine
And to help others do the same,
As I offer up *(whatever your concern or problem here)* to you
For the conversion of sinners
For the forgiveness of sins
In reparation for sins
And for the salvation of souls. Amen.

Oh my Jesus, I offer this for love of Thee,
for the conversion of sinners,
and in reparation for the sins committed against the
Immaculate Heart of Mary. Amen.

BLESSED MOTHER AT FATIMA

Chapter 23

Preparation for Death

"You must also be prepared, for at an hour you do not expect, the Son of Man will come."

Luke 12:40

You should live every day as if it was your last. If you do so, you should have no fear of your judgment. It is a natural inclination for man to fear death. If you have neglected God in your lifetime, at your death the demons will pounce all over you putting strife and turmoil in your thoughts. This will cause a turbulent and unhappy death. Now, if you have a loving relationship with our Lord, trusting in His great mercy and forgiveness, your death will be a happy one. How can we know this? Just read the true stories about the great martyrs that faced death in the Roman Coliseum. They not only faced death without fear, but actual bliss, praising our Lord as their bodies were being burned or torn apart by ferocious animals.

KEYS TO HIS KINGDON

One should look on this life as a test for winning eternal salvation. I'm shooting for an A+, what about you?

****

"The proper time for repairing a disordered conscience is not at the hour of death but during life."

ST. ALPHONSUS LIGUORI
Bishop, Doctor of the Church, 1696-1787

"To guide the vessel well, the pilot must place himself at the helm; thus, to lead a good life, a man must always imagine himself in death."

ST. BONAVENTURE
Bishop, Doctor of the Church, 1217-1274

"Look on the sins of youth, and blush; look on the sins of manhood, and weep; look on the present disorders of thy life, and tremble and amend."

"Death may assail you and take away your life in every place and at every time, you should, if you wish to die well and to save your soul, be at all times and places in expectation of death."

ST. BERNARD OF CLAIRVAUX
Abbot, Doctor of the Church, 1090-1153

PREPARATION FOR DEATH

"Begin now what you will be hereafter."

ST. JEROME
Priest, Father and Doctor of the Church, 1347-1420

"It is true, that at whatsoever hour the sinner is converted, God promises to pardon him; but He has not said that in death sinners will be converted; on the contrary, He has often declared that he who live in sin shall die in sin. "You shall die in your sins." (John, 8: 21-24). He has said that they who seek Him at the hour of death shall not find Him. "You shall seek me and shall not find me." (John, 7:34). We must, then, seek God when he may be found." (Isaias. 55:6). Yes, because a time will come when He will not be found. Poor blind sinners! Poor blind ones! who wait to be converted till the hour of death, when there will be no more time for conversion."

ST. ALPHONSUS LIGUORI
Bishop, Doctor of the Church, 1696-1787

"Take care of your body as if you were going to live forever; and take care of your soul as if you were going to die tomorrow."

ST. AUGUSTINE
Bishop, Father and Doctor of the Church, 354-430

KEYS TOHIS KINGDON

"O unhappy sinners, do not rely upon the greatness of God's Mercy; believe me, the more you provoke the anger of this merciful God by willful sin, the deeper you will be cast into the abyss of perdition."

ST. CATHERINE OF SIENA
Doctor of the Church, Stigmatic, Mystic, 1347-1380

"Every action of yours, every thought, should be those of one who expects to die before the day is out. Death would have no great terrors for you if you had a quiet conscience...Then why not keep clear of sin instead of running away from death? If you aren't fit to face death today, it's very unlikely you will be tomorrow...." *The Imitation of Christ.*

THOMAS A KEMPAS
Priest, 1380-1471

Prayer for Preparation for Death

Eternal Father, for the love of Jesus Christ. Give me holy perseverance and the grace to love Thee, and to love Thee greatly during the remainder of my life. O Mary, Mother of mercy, by the love thou bearest thy Jesus, obtain for me these two graces, perseverance and love. Amen.

Chapter 24

Death and Judgment

*"For we must all appear before the judgment
seat of Christ, so that each one may receive
recompense, according to what he did in the body,
weather good or evil."*

2 Corinthians 5: 10

The Church teaches that the soul receives two judgments. The first one takes place at the death of our body and is called the particular judgment. This is when we are judged by Jesus and sent either to Heaven, Purgatory, or Hell. The second judgment takes place at the end of the world when Christ returns to judge all mankind. It is at this judgment that our soul will be reunited with our glorified body. The Catechism teaches us, "It is Jesus Himself who on the last day will raise up

KEYS TO HIS KINGDOM

those who have believed in him, who have eaten his body and drunk his blood." (CCC 994).

****

"For the just He will come in love, for the wicked in terror."

"O amiable death, who is he that desires thee not, since thou art the termination of troubles, the end of labor, the beginning of eternal repose."

ST. AUGUSTINE
Bishop, Father and Doctor of the Church, 354-430

"Death is not only the end of labors, but it is also the gate of life."

ST. BERNARD OF CLAIRVAUX
Abbot, Doctor of the Church, 1090-1153

"Our death ought not to be called death, but the beginning of life."

ST. BRUNO
Priest, 1030-1101

"Rejoice with me, for I quit the land of sorrows, and I go to a place of peace."

ST. CATHERINE OF SIENA
Doctor of the Church, Stigmatic, Mystic, 1347-1380

DEATH AND JUDGEMENT

"We should all realize that no matter where or how a man dies, if he is in the state of mortal sin and does not repent, when he could have done so and did not, the Devil tears his soul from his body with such anguish and distress that only a person who has experienced it can appreciate it."

"Let us have charity and humility, and give alms, for almsgiving cleanses our souls from the filth of sin. At death we lose all that we have in this world, but we take with us charity and the alms and deeds we have done, and for these we shall receive a great reward from God."

ST. FRANCES OF ASSISI
Friar, Mystic, Stigmatic, 1181-1226

"And so man separated himself from the fruit of all good things, and by his disobedience he was filled with the fruit that brings destruction. And the name of that fruit was mortal sin Straightway he died to the more perfect life: he passed from a divine life to one on the level with irrational beasts. Once death was mingled with his nature, mortality was passed on to all generations of his children. Hence we are born into a life of death, for, in a certain sense, our very life has died. Our life is indeed dead because we have been deprived of immortality. But the man who is aware that he lives in the midst of two lives can cross the barrier between them, such that by destroying the one he can give the victory to the other. Man by his death to the true life entered into this life of death. So too, when he dies to this irrational life of death, he is restored to life eternal. And so there is no doubt but that we cannot enter into this life of blessedness unless we die to sin."

ST GREGORY OF NYSSA
Bishop, 335-394

"As the Lord thought good so it came to pass. Let us adopt those marvelous words. At the hands of the righteous Judge, they who show like good deeds shall receive a like reward....He whom we love is not hidden in the ground; he is received into heaven. Let us wait a little while, and we shall be once more with him. The time of our separation is not long, for in this life we are all like travelers on a journey, hastening on to the same shelter. While one has reached his rest another arrives, another hurries on but one and the same end awaits them all."

ST. BASIL THE GREAT
Father and Doctor of the Church, 330-379

"If we were required to die twice, we could jettison one death. But man dies once only, and upon this death depends his eternity. Where the tree falls, there it shall lie. If, at the hour of death, someone is living in bad habit, the poor soul will fall on the side of hell. If, on the other hand, he is in the state of grace, it will take the road for heaven. Oh, happy road!"

ST. JOHN VIANNEY
Priest, 1786-1859

DEATH AND JUDGEMENT

"It is not Death that will come to fetch me, it is the good God. Death is no phantom, no horrible specter, as presented in pictures. In the catechism it is stated that death is the separation of soul and body, that is all! Well, I am not afraid of a separation which will unite me to the good God forever."

ST. THERESE OF LISIEUX
Nun, Doctor of the Church, 1873-1897

"How consoling it is to see a just man die! His death is good, because it ends his miseries; it is better still, because he begins a new life; it is excellent, because it places him in sweet security. From this bed of mourning, whereon he leaves a precious load of virtues, he goes to take possession of the true land of the living, Jesus acknowledges him as His brother and as His friend, for he has died to the world before closing his eyes from its dazzling light. Such is the death of the saints, a death very precious in the sight of God."

ST. BERNARD OF CLAIRVAUX
Abbot, Doctor of the Church, 1090-1153

"I do not know a greater happiness than to die for Jesus Christ, or for the salvation of my neighbor."

ST. IGNATIUS OF LOYOLA
Priest, Mystic, Founder of the Jesuits, 1491-1556

KEYS TO HIS KINGDOM

"In the meditation on death, I asked the Lord to deign to fill my heart with those sentiments which I will have at the moment of my death. And through God's grace I received an interior reply that I had done what was within my power and so could be at peace. At that moment, such profound gratitude to God was awakened in my soul that I burst into tears of joy like a little child. I prepared to receive Holy Communion next morning as "viaticum," and I said the prayers of the dying for my own intention.

"Then I heard the words: As you are united with Me in life, so will you be united at the moment of death. After these words, such great trust in God's great mercy was awakened in my soul that, even if I had had the sins of the whole world, as well as the sins of all the condemned souls weighing on my conscience, I would not have doubted God's goodness but, without hesitation, would have thrown myself into the abyss of the divine mercy, which is always open to us; and, with a heart crushed to dust, I would have cast myself at His feet, abandoning myself totally to His holy will, which is mercy itself." *Divine Mercy in My Soul*, Notebook V, (1551-1552).

ST. FAUSTINA
Sister, Mystic, "Secretary of Divine Mercy", 1905-1938

"When once you have departed this life, there is no longer any place for repentance, no way of making satisfaction. Here life is either lost or kept. Here, by the worship of God and by the fruit of faith, provision is made for eternal salvation. Let no one be kept back either

DEATH AND JUDGEMENT

by his sins or by his years from coming to obtain salvation. To him who still remains in this world there is no repentance that is too late."

ST. CYPRIAN OF CARTHAGE
Bishop, Martyr, 210-258

"Man acts so far as he can in accordance with his own wishes; but God decides the outcome in accordance with justice."

ST. MARK THE ASCETIC
Monk, 360-430

"Precious in the sight of the Lord is the death of his saints." Psalms 15:15.

"Now, observe, my daughter, the contrast between the luxurious dress of many women, and the raiment and adornments of Jesus. . . Tell me: what relation do their fine shoes bear to the spikes in Jesus' Feet? The rings on their hands to the nails which perforated His? The fashionable coiffure to the Crown of Thorns? The painted face to That covered with bruises? Shoulders exposed by the low-cut gown to His, all striped with Blood? Ah, but there is a marked likeness between these worldly women and the Jews who, incited by the Devil, scourged Our Lord! At the hour of such a woman's death, I think Jesus will be heard saying: "Cujus est imago haec et circumscripto. . . of whom is she the image?" And the reply will be: "Demonii... of the Devil!" Then He will say: "Let her who has followed the Devil's fashions be handed over to him; and to God, those who have imitated the modesty of Jesus and Mary."[4]

ST. ANTHONY MARY CLARET
Archbishop, Missionary,1807-1870

---

[4] A Very Special Patron: Saint Anthony Mary Claret Catholicism.ORG.

Closing Prayer

My beloved Jesus, during the remaining years of my life, give me strength to do something for Thee, ere death comes upon me. Give me strength against my temptations and passions, especially against that passion which in the past has caused me to displease Thee. Give me patience under infirmities, and under the injuries that I may receive from men, I now pardon, for the love of Thee, all who have shown me any contempt, and I beseech Thee to grant them the grace they desire. Give me strength to be more diligent in avoiding even venial sin, in regard of which I know myself to be careless. My Savior, help me; I hope for all through Thy merits; and I confide all to thy intercession, O Mary, my Mother, and my hope. I ask this not with my will but in God's Will. Amen.

Acknowledgments

I would like to acknowledge the following books, organizations, and websites which I used in gathering some of the quotes that I have used in this book. The quotations taken from the following sources have been copied under public domain or under the Fair Use Doctrine, codified in 17 U.S.C. 107.

CATECHISM OF THE CATHOLIC CHURCH.

THE NEW AMERICAN BIBLE.

DOUAY-RHEIMS, THE HOLY BIBLE.

THE SERMONS OF ST. ALPHONSUS LIGUORI For All the Sundays of the Year, Tan Books. ISBN 978-0-89555-193-1.

TRUE DEVOTION TO MARY, St. Louis De Monfort Translated by Fr. Frederick Faber, Tan Books. ISBN0-89555-279-5.

SAINT MARIA FAUSTINA KOWALSKI DIARY, Divine Mercy in My Soul, Marian Press. ISBN 978-1-59614-189-6.

PREPARATION FOR DEATH, A Popular Abridgement, St. Alphonsus Liguori Tan Books. ISBN 978-0-89555-174-0.

CATHOLIC ANSWERS, www.catholic.com.

ALL ABOUT THE ANGELS, Fr. Paul O'Sullivan, O.P. Tan Books. ISBN 978-0-89555-388-1.

MANUAL FOR SPIRITUAL WARFARE. Paul Thigpen, Tan Books. ISBN 978-1-61890-653-3.

SERMONS OF THE CURE of ARS, translated by UNA MORRISSY, Tan Books. ISBN 0-89555-524-7.

THE LIFE & TIMES OF SAINT BERNARD, Fr. Theodore Ratisbonne, Caritos Publishing. ISBN 9781945275081.

PURGATORY, Explained By The Lives and Legends of The Saints, Fr. F. X. Schouppe, S. J. Tan Books. ISBN 0-89555-831-9.

DELIVERANCE PRAYERS, For Use By The Laity, Sensus Traditionis Press. ISBN 9781541056718.

IN SEARCH OF TRUTH, A Layman's Guide to Catholic Spirituality, Hickory Hill Press. ISBN 9780983915829.

THE CATHOLIC READER, A Devotional Blog for Catholics, thecatholicreader.blogspot.com.

EPIC PEW, epicpew.com.

AMC4L, amcatholic4life.com.

Other Books by the Author.

In Search of Truth: *A Layman's Guide to Catholic Spirituality.* It has been granted the Nihil Obstat and Imprimatur by the Catholic Church.
ISBN 9780983915829

My Daily Prayer Book, ISBN 978-0983915850

Rattler One-Seven, *A Vietnam Helicopter Pilot's War Story.* University of North Texas Press ISBN- 13 978-1-57441-221-5

First Light, *A POWs Rescue Mission That Can Never Be Acknowledged.* ISBN 9780983915805

Excerpts From Luisa, ISBN 9780983915843